ABOUT THE COVER IMAGE

The USCGC Courier (WTR-410) served as a mobile barracks and operational training platform for training Coast Guard Reserves from 1966 to 1972. The Courier supported various Port Security Unites training at major ports on the East coast, Gulf of Mexico, and the Great Lakes.

Before training Reservist, the Courier was stationed in Roads, Greece from July 1952 to August 1964. The ship was fitted with a high-powered transmitter and operated as a relay station for "Voice of America."

COUNTRY BOY GOES TO SEA

MY YEARS IN THE U.S. COAST GUARD

By: **M. LEON BEATY**

LCDR, USCG (Retired)

authorHOUSE®

AuthorHouse™
1663 Liberty Drive
Bloomington, IN 47403
www.authorhouse.com
Phone: 833-262-8899

Published by AuthorHouse 02/27/2023

ISBN: 979-8-8230-0051-2 (sc)
ISBN: 979-8-8230-0050-5 (e)

Print information available on the last page.

This book is printed on acid-free paper.

ROADWAYS

By John Masefield

One road leads to London,
  One road leads to Wales,
My road leads me seawards
  To the white dipping sails.

One road leads to the river,
  As it goes singing slow,
My road leads to shipping,
  Where the bronzed sailor go.

Leads me, lures me, calls me
  To salt green tossing sea,
A road without earth's road-dust
  Is the right road for me.

A wet road heaving, shining,
  And wild with seagulls' cries.
A mad salt sea-wind blowing
  The salt spray in my eyes.

My road calls me, lures me
  West, east, south, and north.
Most roads lead men homewards,
  My road leads me forth

To add more miles to the tally
  Of grey miles left behind,
In quest of that one beauty
  God put me here to find.

CONTENTS

ACKNOWLEDGEMENTS

Following are my memories of my 20 years in the U.S. Coast Guard from August 4, 1959, to September 30, 1979. These recollections are primarily for my children and grandchildren. Since 40 plus years have passed, some of the details have faded. The facts are a little fuzzy, but I have recorded them the best of my ability. If there are errors to some of the details, chalk them up to old age.

I very much enjoyed my time in the service. The structure of military service fit my personality just fine. I got to fulfill my need for adventure. Ever since I was a young boy I wanted to be around ships and the sea. Somewhere along the line I decided I wanted to be an officer in a seagoing service. While my life did not go as I expected, God allowed me to reach that goal when the time was right.

I meet a lot of nice people in the Coast Guard and was able to see a lot of the United States of America. If a person does not know what they want to do after high school, I would encourage them to spend a tour of duty in the military.

After leaving the Coast Guard I had difficulty adjusting. I spent a lot of time jumping around from one job to another. I worked as a supervisor in a factory, helped build a house, worked in the oil fields, drove a truck, worked retail, and ran the office for a small construction company. What gave me the most pleasure was volunteering in the small town where I settled down.

I hope you enjoy reading the following as much as I did reminiscing.

God bless!!

Marvin Leon Beaty
LCDR, USCG, (Retired)

CHAPTER 1

THE EARLY YEARS

When I traveled from Kansas City, Missouri to Cape May, New Jersey, it was the first time I had traveled east of the Mississippi river. You would think that I would remember how I traveled for an occasion like that. For the life of me I have no memory of that trip. It was 1959 and I had just enlisted in the U.S. coast Guard, and I was traveling to Cape May, NJ for boot camp. I was 18 years old.

I grew up in Pawnee, a small rural town in north central Oklahoma. When I was in about the fifth grade, I developed an interested in reading. I read the usual adventure and mystery stories for young people such as The Hardy Boys, and Tom Swift. One of my favored series of books was C. S. Forester's, the Horatio Hornblower series. I was always interested in sailing ships and other sea stories.

When I was a junior in high school, I decided I would like a career that had something to do with the sea. I researched and studied all the information I could get about the Navy and the Merchant Marine. I decided that I did not want to be on a large ship like a battleship or aircraft carrier, so I ruled the Navy out.

My English teacher that year was a Navy veteran. I discussed my interest with him. He had been stationed at a Navy base in Groton Connecticut. Across the river was the Coast Guard Academy in New London, CT. He suggested that I research the Coast Guard since that seemed to fit my interest. We had to write a paper for class that year, so my topic was the U.S. Coast Guard. After researching and writing that term paper I knew what I wanted to do after high school.

What interested me most was the fact the Coast Guard had a full-time peace time mission. Sure, the Coast Guard had a military mission. It had been in every war since its first origins as the Revenue Marine in 1790. The Coast Guard peace time missions of maritime safety, search and rescue, fisheries patrol, environmental pretention, drug interdiction, aids to navigation and port security appealed to me. Who am I trying to kid, I just wanted to go to sea for the adventure.

My junior year, early 1957, I applied for the Coast Guard Academy. You did not have to have a Congressional appointment like the other military academies. The appointment was based on how well you did on written test given each year. Since I lived in land locked Oklahoma, I did not thank there would be many people applying to take the test. Boy was I wrong! I had to travel to Oklahoma City, about 100 miles, for the exam. When I walked into the exam room there must have been 75 to 100 people setting for the exam.

Later that summer of 1957, I received a letter from the Coast Guard. I did not score high enough on the exam to earn a spot at the Academy. I was in a blue funk mood for several days. I finished high school in 1958 and moved on with my life.

I wanted to enlist in the Coast Guard after high school, but I was only 17. Since I was not 18, I needed my father's signature to join. He would not sign, because he wanted me to go to college. My older brother, Otis, had quit high school early and after he was 18, joined the Army.

To please my father, I went to Oklahoma State University in the fall of 1958. I had been interested in building things, so I enrolled in a two-year course called Building Construction Technology. The curriculum covered such things as carpentry, masonry, architectural drafting and the usual english and math.

My Mon and Dad paid the tuition and books, but I had to get a job to have money for living expenses. I found a job washing dishes at an off-campus eatery that catered to college students. The building was a little run down, but the food was good and served family style. I got to eat for free and was paid a small salary. I earned enough to live on and had plenty of time to study.

For my first semester the school required that I lived in a dorm on campus. It was close to most of my classes. A lot of classes were in classrooms under the stadium for the football field. I was not very good at taking notes, however my memory was excellent, so I was able to get good grades on my exams. I did well in school and carried a B average.

The second semester the rules allowed me to live off campus. I rented a room from an older lady in a home south of campus. There were three other students living there. It was further to go to classes and work, but I liked the freedom. There was less structure and rules than at the dorm.

This semester one of my classes was architectural drafting. I really enjoyed the class and did well until the final assignment. I was supposed to design a high-end home with unlimited funds to build. I just could not get interested in the project. At the end of the semester, I received a grade of incomplete because I had not turned in the blueprints. The instructor told me that if I finished the drawings during the summer my grade would change to a "B". even with the extra time, I still did not finish the assignment.

Between my part time job and studying for my classes I did not have a lot of time for socializing. I did spend some time attending activities at the Baptist Student Center off campus. I noticed that there were two major categories of students living in the dorm. Those that spent a lot of time drinking and partying, and the ones had their nose in the books until wee hours of the night. The ones that spent their time studying were usually older students attending school on the G.I. Bill.

The summer of 1959, my teachers helped me get a summer job with a local construction company there in Stillwater. OK. The job was not much. I was the office gofer. I sweep the floors, emptied the trash cans, and filed. I wanted to work at a job site, not sit around in an office. I was not happy with my job, had lost interest in school, so I decided to join the Coast Guard. Since I was 18 now, I could join the service on my own. My Dad was not happy with my decision. I moved my belongings back home to Pawnee, OK.

I contacted the Coast Guard recruiting office in ST. Louis, MO and got the paperwork started. The Recruiter told me that I would have to go to Kansas City, MO to take a physical. If I passed the physical, then I would sign up and head for boot camp without going back home. I packed a small bag, caught the Greyhound buss and headed for Kansas City. Coast Guard here I come.

CHAPTER 2

BOOT CAMP

I enlisted in the Coast Guard on August 4, 1959, in Kansas City, MO. I learned later that August 4th was considered the Coast Guard birthday. I traveled to Cape May, NJ to go to boot camp. As I stated previously, I don't remember how I traveled to Cape May. However, thinking back to travel options available at that time, I probably travel by train or bus. I would have gone to Chicago and then to Philadelphia, PA. From there I would have gone by bus to the Coast Guard Station.

The boot camp at Cape May was located on old air station. The barracks were two story wooden buildings left over from World War II. The administration building and some of the classrooms were brick. There was a base exchange, a mess hall (better known as chow hall), a large, enclosed swimming pool and other support buildings.

As we got off the bus we were assigned to a receiving barracks until everyone arrived. When about 30 recruits had arrived, we were met by a drill instructor, a chief petty officer. He proceeded to chew us up one side and down the other. The drill instructor (or

DI) and his assistant, a 1st class petty officer, would be with us for the rest of our stay at boot camp. We learned to stand up straight, line up in formation and march from one location to another.

Bootcamp at that time was an eight-week program. We spent the first week getting settled in, eight weeks training and the last week getting processed for our first duty station.

That first week, while we were getting organized, in our off hours some of us were assigned to KP (kitchen patrol). On KP we would wash pots and pans, bring food, or supplies from the storeroom to the kitchen, mop floors, or anything else the cooks needed. Those recruits not on KP were kept busy policing the area near the barracks. "Policing the area" meant picking up cigarette buts and trash. The cigarettes had to be "field striped" which consisted of shredding the filters on cigarettes. The DI could always find something to keep us busy and our minds off home.

That week we were herded into the barber shop for haircuts. We then marched from this building to that building to receive our uniforms, bedding, books, and other gear we would need during the next eight weeks. Civilian clothes were packed up and mailed home. We were issued an M1 Grand rifle to carry around until we graduated.

The second week we had been organized into a platoon of about 30 recruits. The platoon was assigned to either the first or second floor of a barracks building. The DI or his assistant stayed in a separate room at one end of the squad bay. Across from him was the latrine, (bathroom). We got up early in the morning for group exercises, and then it was back to the squad room for showers. Next, we marched to the chow hall for breakfast. After breakfast we had a few minutes to ourselves, and then it was march to this class, or that class, or close order drill, or whatever was on the orders for the day.

Boot camp was not what I expected. Sure, there was a lot of close order drill, early morning exercise and that sort of thing. But there was more classroom training than I expected. We had class on seamanship, tying knots, Coast Guard history, first aid and many other topics. I can remember going to a classroom and learning how to "field strip" (take it apart) the M-1 Grand rifle, cleaning it and putting the rifle back together. After we learned to take care of our rifle (it's not a gun), we went out to the parade grounds to learn close order drill. Close order drill taught us the commands and how to march with a rifle.

We spent a lot of time on the parade grounds, i.e., drill field or grinder. The DI would yell and scream at you when you made a mistake during close order drill. If you made the same mistake three or four times, then the DI would make you run at "high port" around the grinder. High port consisted of running with your 9.5-pound M1 rifle held over your head. 9.5 pounds does not sound like a lot, but it gets heavy real fast.

I did not know it at the time, but I had dyslexia, which means I had a hard time telling my right from my left. When the DI gave a command of column right, I would turn left. This would happen a lot. As a result, I spent a lot of time running at high port around the grinder. I became well acquainted with the drill field.

Something that I did not like was the classes at the indoor swimming pool. I had not learned to swim; therefore, I was not comfortable during our water classes. During WW II there were a lot of times when you had to abandon ship by jumping over the side. You can get hurt bad by jumping the incorrect way. To learn to jump the correct way we had to put on life jackets "the correct way" and then jump off the 30-foot-high dive into the water. I found out that I did not like heights, especially jumping off into thin air. It was extremely hard for me to jump off the high dive. It was a good thing they did not have a "grinder" at the pool. I would have spent a lot of time there.

One thing I wanted to do was run the obstacle course. Unfortunately, the obstacle course was in disrepair and need a lot of work to get it into shape. When our class time came to run the course, it was under construction. We also did not get as much time on the small boats as I would like. I spent too much time on the grinder.

During the first five weeks in the evening, during the week, we were restricted to the barracks except when we were on guard duty or on KP. We were supposed to study our lessons, write letters home, and keep our uniforms and rifles clean. On the weekend we could go to the Base Exchange. There we could make telephone calls home, buy books, candy, soda, and other small items we needed. It was nice to get away from the rest of the platoon and the barracks.

Starting week six we could get a day pass to leave the base. A pass was privilege if you had been good during the past week. If you flunked test on classroom material, did bad during close order drill, or otherwise upset the DI, then you were restricted to the base. While on pass you could go into Cape May, NJ or go to Wildwood, NJ which was the next town to the North. Wildwood had a boardwalk and a nice beach. The guys liked to go there to see if they could get a date with the girls. It was sure nice to get away from the base for a day. Later, sometimes, you could get a weekend pass.

During our ninth week (eighth week of training) General George C. Marshal, 5-star General of the Army, died on October

16, 1959. Because of his positions as Chief of Staff of the Army and later Secretary of Defense he was given a special military funeral in Washington, D.C. For part of the ceremony, he was laid in state at Washington National Cathedral on October 19 & 20, 1959. Part of ceremony was the Joint Honor Guard made up of Army, Air Force, Marines, Navy, Coast Guard, and a cadet from the Virginia Military Institute. Our platoon was chosen to go to Washington, D.C. to provide personnel for the Coast Guard portion of the ceremony. I was part of the joint honor guard for the casket during the night of October 19th. The next day was the funeral and a precession from the Cathedral to Arlington National Cemetery.

Upon returning from Washington, D.C. it was time for the Graduation Parade. Thank goodness I turned right when the DI commanded "column right". No MORE high port around the grinder. I advanced from Seaman Recruit, (E-1), to Seaman Apprentice, (E-2). We had to turn in our M1 rifle, our bedding and other gear. Our uniforms and everything we owned was packed in a standard military duffel bag. It is surprising how much will fit in a duffel bag if packed properly.

Next came processing for our next duty station. I was assigned to the Commander, Fifth Coast Guard District, Portsmouth, VA for further assignment. We were given ten days leave and travel time before reporting to our next duty station. I was going to travel back to my home in Oklahoma before reporting in.

One of my classmates, Norman Cherry, was also going to the Fifth District. He invited me to stop by his house in Portsmouth, VA and we would report in together. I accepted his offer and made plans to meet him at his home when my leave was over. Then I caught a Greyhound bus and headed for home.

CHAPTER 3

USCGC *CHINCOTEAGUE* (WAVP-375)

In early November 1959, I returned from 10 days leave and travel time. My orders were to report to the Personnel Office, Fifth Coast Guard District, Portsmouth, VA for reassignment. My classmate, Norman Cherry, and I had the same orders. He suggested that I come to his home, and we would go to the District Office together. He had given me his telephone number and address.

Upon arriving in Portsmouth, VA, I called Norman. His Mother, Francis Bland, answered the phone and said that Norman was off visiting friends. She told me to come on over and gave me directions. Upon arriving at Norman's home, I was nervous about meeting people that I did not know. Norman lived in a nice suburban neighborhood, but I was too shy to go up to the door. I was pacing the sidewalk across the street, in uniform, for about 10 minutes. I must have stood out like sore thumb. Then a cute 15-year-old girl, Linda Cherry, my future wife, came across the street and asks if I was Leon. When I said yes, she said come in and meet the family. I was introduced to Norman's Mother, Frances

Bland, his Stepdad, Bill Bland, and two younger brothers, Billy, and Buck.

The next day Norman and I went to the District Office and reported in. Norman was assigned to a shore station in Baltimore, MD. I was assigned to the USCGC *Chincoteague* (WAVP-275) whose home port was at the Coast Guard Base in Norfolk, VA.

The *Chincoteague's* primary duty was manning Ocean Stations in the North Atlantic. An Ocean Station was one of several weather patrol areas off the coast of Greenland and Iceland. Our job was to stay on station for weather reporting, search and rescue and oceanographic research. While on station we also acted as aircraft check point, at the point of no return, for trans-Atlantic flights. While on duty in one of these stations, the cutter was required to patrol a 210 square mile area for three weeks at a time, leaving the area only when physically relieved by another Coast Guard cutter on in the case of a dire emergency.

The CGC *Chincoteague* had been built as a Navy seaplane tender during WWII. After the war she was loaned to the Coast Guard. We had a crew of 149 (10 Officers, 3 Warrant Officers and 136 enlisted personnel). When on Ocean Station (Weather Patrol)

duty there were also four civilian weathermen from NOAA on board. The cutter was 210 ft. long, 41 ft. wide with a draft of 12 ft. Our cruising speed was 11.5 knots, with max speed of 17.0 knots in an emergency. For armament there was a single 5-inch cannon, two 40-mm duel barrel anti-aircraft guns and depth charge projectors.

Upon reporting aboard for duty, I was assigned to the deck force. We had our own berthing area in the aft part of the ship. Personnel working in the engine room (black gang) lived in a separate area. Petty officers in the Operations department also had a separate berthing area.

The berthing area consisted of three 2 ft. 6 inches wide by 6 ft. long steel frame bunks one above the other. There were two tears of bunks back-to-back with a column 0f 2 ft. by 2ft. lockers at the end. Each person was assigned a locker for clothing and personal gear. Anything that didn't fit in the locker was left in the duffel bag which was stowed below. This was my home for the next eight months.

The ship's crew was divided into three duty sections. When in port (tied up to the dock) one section would have the "duty" (stay on board when liberty granted) and the other two could go ashore on liberty. During the day from 8 a.m. to about 5 p.m. the crew would clean the ship, perform repairs and maintenance work, and take care of duties in their various specialties. When on liberty you could do just about anything you wanted as long as you were back aboard by 8 o'clock the next day, sober and ready to work.

My job on the Deck Force was to do whatever the third-class boatswain's mate told me to do. This included washing (swabbing) down the decks, chipping rust and then painting where we had chipped. The salt spray caused everything to rust so there was always something to chip and paint.

On one occasion the ship started coming up short on paint brushes. It seems men would throw used paint brushes over the side instead of cleaning and return them to the paint locker. The Chief Boas'n called the deck force together and really chewed us out. He said that the next seaman that didn't return a paint brush would lose his liberty for a week.

A short time later two men were on a float, in the water, painting the side of the ship. A ship came by and caused a large wake. The rough waves caused the men on the float to fall in the water. One of them resurfaced, sputtering, holding his paint brush straight up above his head. He was yelling "I didn't lose the brush; I didn't lose the brush."

When in port I would stand messenger watch on the quarterdeck and run errands as needed. When we were underway, I would stand lookout watches or bridge messenger and later be a helmsman and steer the ship.

There was an organization chart called "Watch Quarter and Station Bill". Everyone on the cutter was assigned a job which was different depending on what activity was going on, i.e. anchor detail, fire, man overboard, battle stations etc. When leaving or arriving in port I was with the anchor detail on the bow. My job was telephone talker. I would relay messages to the bridge and back. At battle stations I was loader on the port (left) 40mm dual mount gun.

The officer in charge of the deck force had the title of "First Lieutenant." His name LT John O'Malley but we all called him "the Coach". Instead of just giving orders like other officers, he would gather us around and tell us what we needed to do and why it had to be done a certain way. Kind of like a football coach.

A couple of weeks after reporting aboard, as one of the new men on board, I was assigned "mess cook" duty for a month. Being a mess cook was like KP at boot camp. You washed pots and pans, peeled potatoes, fetched supplies from the storage lockers in the bottom of the ship. One week I was assigned mess cook duties in the Chief's berthing area. There I was to clean the area, empty the trash cans and whatever else needed to be done. One thing I did was scrub the inside of the coffee pot. It looked pretty dirty to me. I got chewed out by every chief petty officer on board. You do not clean the coffee pot. Coffee does not taste the same afterward I was told. How would I know, I did not drink coffee!

Peeling potatoes was not hard once you got the hang of the job. You put the potatoes in this round machine that looked like it had really course sandpaper inside. The machine would spin the batch of potatoes taking most of the skin off. After the potatoes came out of the machine you had to cut the eyes out by hand. You had to be careful not to leave the potatoes in too long. They would come out small. Then the cook would chew you out because he did not have enough potatoes to serve.

Another mess cook duty was to paint the walls of the storage lockers. The lockers were small rooms in the bottom of the ship. There was no place to put the paint roller tray except on the floor. Not paying attention to what I was doing, what did I do? I stepped into the paint tray, and then I proceeded to get paint steps all over the floor. That just wasn't my day.

When we got underway it took us three or four days to get to the Ocean Station we were assigned. Usually, we stopped at the

Navy base in Argentina, Newfangled to top off the fuel tanks. This was an overnight stop. We were granted liberty but could not leave the U.S. Navy Base. The tides were very high in this area, about 40 feet. We had to enter and leave port only on high tide.

Weather in the North Atlantic was very changeable, especially during the winter months. On calm days we could just drift in our patrol area. When a storm came up, the waves would build up and we would have to steam into the wind and sea to stay in our patrol area.

During the winter months, in heavy seas, the water would break over the bow. In really rough weather we would take what was called green water. This would mean that there was solid water as well as spray coming onboard. Sometimes the water and spray went as high as the bridge. The bridge was three decks above the main deck and almost one quarter of the way back from the bow.

During the winter the salt spray would freeze on the topside superstructure. When the ice got too thick, the extra weight would cause the ship to become top heavy. Too much ice and the ship could capsize. When the ice started getting thick, we would have to go out on deck with baseball bats and hammers and break ice. That was a very cold job and not much fun.

Life, when we were underway, was very much a routine. I would stand watches four hours on and eight hours off. As a seaman apprentice I would stand lookout watch either on the bow or on the bridge wing. In rough weather both lookouts were on the bridge. With water breaking over the bow it was too dangerous to have a lookout on the forecastle. During the daytime, 8 to 5, when not on watch we would do ship maintenance work. Off duty hours were spent sleeping, reading, watching movies, or just hanging out.

If you stood midnight to four watches on the bridge, the cook would bring up midnight rations (mid-rats). Other departments had to go to the mess hall to get their chow. One night the cook brought up pizza for mid-rats. The crust was at least two inches thick. It was more like cake with tomato sauce for icing. I had never eaten pizza before, so I did not know what to expect. From listening to the comments of others I knew this pizza was unusual. The cook said it was Chicago style pizza.

When the Captain wanted to have a training drill, it would be announced over the intercom. Something like, "This is a drill, man overboard, abandon ship fire on board or general quarters, man your battle station" would be the call. One evening when we were under way, about dark, I was lying in my rack. Someone came running through the berthing area yelling "Fire, fire in the engine room, man your damage control stations." I thought, yea right, this is a prank. If it was for real, they would announce it over the intercom. However, it was for real. The fire was in the electrical switch board and that caused the inter-com to be out of order. The fire was put out quickly with very little damage, so we continued our patrol.

It took us longer to return to home port in Portsmouth than it did going to the patrol area. It seemed like every trip, about 24 hours out, we would get a SAR call (Search and Rescue). We would have to turn around and steam toward wherever the distress call originated. This extra time came out of our in-port time. Usually someone else would get there first, then we would turn around and head back home. One time we arrived on scene where a merchant ship had lost her propeller. Since the seas were relative calm, we just stood by for two days waiting for a commercial tug to come and tow the ship to port. If the weather had turned bad, the *Chincoteague* would have taken the ship in tow.

Once we arrived in port, the routine was to get ready to go back to Ocean Station again. Two or three days after tying up (mooring), there would be a parade of trucks bringing food, spare parts, and other necessary items. When the food trucks arrived, we would hear the call, "all hands-on deck to resupply." Everything had to be hand carried on board by hand and down to the storage lockers.

The part I liked best was bringing onboard fresh bread. A couple of loaves would be liberated for consumption after all hand's evolution. Frozen bread is good, but eating fresh light bread, after four or five weeks of frozen bread, is like eating ice cream.

On one occasion, instead on going on Ocean Patrol, we pulled a SAR standby in Bermuda. We sailed to St. George, Bermuda which is on the opposite end of the island from Hamilton, the capital. We had to stay ready in case we received an emergency SAR call, but we could go on liberty in a foreign port. The ship was in St. George for three weeks.

There were a lot of historic buildings and places to visit. I enjoyed watching people drive on the wrong side of the road and the way they talked. The money was different also. I had a good time collecting half-pennies which were the size of an American half dollar.

All the houses were painted bright pastel colors. They were designed so that rainwater would drain into underground cisterns. There is no underground water or wells on the island. All the household water had to come from rainwater. Fortunately, it rained often in Bermuda.

Another out of the ordinary trip was a visit to Guantanamo Bay, Cuba. The U.S. Navy had a large base there. We went there for what was called "refresher training." The ship would put out to sea every day and Navy observers would grade us on how well we did on various drills. The idea was to sharpen our skills and get us ready for all emergencies.

Even though we had a full-time peace time mission, we were still a military organization and had to be ready for a national emergency or war. This was the only time that I got to help fire the 40 mm anti-aircraft guns. An aircraft would fly over pulling a banner on a long line. Our job was to try to hit the banner. As a loader, my job was to load four round clips of ammunition into one of the two barrels. You had to remain calm and put the clip in the correct way. If you got excited and, in a hurry, you would load the ammunition chip incorrectly and cause the gun to jamb.

When the ship was in port the CGC *Chincoteague* moored at the Coast Guard Base, Norfolk, VA. The Coast Guard Base was located on east side of the Elizabeth River and was just across the river from the Norfolk Naval Shipyard, which was in Portsmouth, VA. Portsmouth and Norfolk, VA were sister cities located were the Elizabeth River and the James River flowed into the Chesapeake Bay.

When I was on liberty, I would often go into downtown Norfolk, VA. Norfolk was just a short city bus ride from where the cutter tied up. We were required to wear uniforms when we left and returned to the ship. We could not keep civilian clothing on board, no room.

Since you had to be in uniform when you left the ship, you would buy civilian clothes then rent a locker by the month to store the clothes in. These places were like a locker room at school. You had a place to change and usually take a shower also. If you wanted to stay out all night, they would rent you a bunk for the night. There would be about 25 or 30 bunks to a room. Just like being back in the barracks again.

In the late 50's and early 60's military personnel were not in good standing with the public at large. I guess there were a lot of drunken soldiers and sailors around. Norfolk, Portsmouth, Virginia Beach, Hampton, and Newport News were just one large metropolitan area. There was, and still is, a very large military presence in the area. It was not unusual to see a sign that said, "Dogs and sailors keep of the grass."

One week the Navy Admiral in command of the area got tired of the way the civilian population complained about all the military personnel. He ordered all the pay officers to pay the sailors in two-dollar bills. The whole area was flooded with two-dollar bills. Every time you received change; you would get a two-dollar bill. After that, the attitude of the public started to change.

Downtown Norfolk was different. Everyone wanted you spend your money in his store. There were restaurants, bars, theaters, clothing and jewelry stores, and places where you could rent a locker or a bunk. Many of the stores had barkers that stood at the entrance to the store. They would try to get you to come into their store if you were in uniform.

After I had been on board for about six months, I was advanced from seaman apprentice to seaman. A short time later the First Lieutenant ask me if I could type. When I told him yes, he asked if I would like a job as yeoman striker. That job would be working in an office instead of working on deck. Sounded like a good idea to me so I said yes. He told me to go talk to the Chief Yeoman.

The duties on a yeoman rating was to type letters and leave papers, make out duty rosters, make entries in personnel records and do the filing. I would work for the Chief Yeoman and his boss the Executive Officer. As a yeoman striker I would be an apprentice yeoman until such time as I could go to Yeoman Class A School.

While striking for yeoman, I did not have to stand underway watches. I would work in the ship's office all day and have the evenings off.

On one weather patrol in the spring of 1960, we were short of watch standers in the Radar Room because someone was sick or on leave. I was called on to fill in the gap on the midnight to 4 a.m. watch. I did not know anything about the radar, but they just needed a warm body. There was not a lot going on in the middle of the night. We very seldom saw another ship in our patrol area. Most of the activity was at the beginning of the watch when we had to tract the midnight weather balloon. The rest of the watch we keep watch on the radar for unusual activity. To break the boredom, watch standers would talk, by radio, to the pilots and stewardess of the trans-Atlantic airplanes.

My best memory of my time on the *Chincoteague* was that patrol after I got off radar watch at 4 a.m. The weather was perfect. There was almost no wind and the seas were calm. The ship would steam up to the windward side of the patrol area and drift down to the opposite side. I would go aft and sit on the fantail and watch the sun come. It was quiet because the engines were turned off and no one else was around, just me and the seagulls. The ship would rock gently on the small waves. I would sit and think about how God put everything together so perfectly.

Many times, when I had liberty, I would go out to Lynda Cherry's home. I got along very well with her mother. Mrs. Bland was a gracious southern lady. She made me feel right at home. I guess she was missing her son and I was missing home. It was a good cure for home sickness. I found that I could talk to her much better than I could talk to my own mother. I did not date Lynda at first since she was only 15, but I hung out with her and her friends, boys and girls.

In July of 1960 I received orders to travel to Groton, CT to go to Yeoman Class A School. This school was 11 months long and I would learn everything I needed to know to advance to YN3. I would be leaving the friends I had met on board the Chincoteague and in Portsmouth, but I was ready for a new adventure.

CHAPTER 4

CLASS "A" SCHOOL

I reported to the U.S. Coast Guard Training Station at Avery Point, Groton, Connecticut in early August 1960. I was to attend the Yeoman, Class "A" School. This school was 12 weeks long and was designed to teach me everything I need to know to advance to Petty Officer third class in the Yeoman rating. There were classes in all phases of personnel regulations, administration procedures, and how and where to find answers to questions that may come up in our duties. We also had classes to help us to improve our typing speed.

Avery Point was a 71-acre site which extends into Long Island Sound at the entrance of the Thames River. It was named after a sea captain who settled the Greater New London area shortly before the turn of the 20th century. New London was at one time the nation's largest whaling port. Today the river front is still bustling with activity, ranging from pleasure boats to nuclear submarines. This area is tremendously important as a center for Coast Guard and Naval training programs. Besides the Training Station, at Groton, the Coast Guard Academy and the Coast Guard Moorings are located on the west bank of the Thames River in New

London. On the east bank is the Navy submarine Base, probably the largest such base in the world. Next to the Navy Base is a shipyard where the build nuclear submarines.

The Avery Point property came into the possession of Morton F. Plant, a successful railroad magnate. Mr. Plant's home was designed and built by architects from Italy and materials were imported from Italian quarries. The "Mansion" (called Branford House) is still on the property and served as the Administration Building for the Training Station. The Coast Guard has historically been saddled with budget shortfalls. In one of the cost saving measures, the Training Station was closed, and the courses are now taught in other locations. It is sad that this beautiful location is no longer a part of the Coast Guard family.

The Training Station's primary function was to graduate trained and qualified Coast Guardsmen in the specialties need for the efficient operation of the Service. Of the 44 basic rates in the Coast Guard, schools for 12 of them were located at Avery Point. For other rates, such as those in the aviation branch, the Coast Guard utilized the facilities of Navy schools.

The length of the courses varied from 2 to 32 weeks, depending upon the nature of the subjects taught. These courses included gunnery, machinery, damage control, administrative, clerical, and financial work, storekeeper, electricity, commissary, and radar. In addition to the basic schools there were 4 advanced Class "C" schools for enlisted men. There were also several specialty schools. The Training Station was also used by Coast Guard Reservists who were completing their final phase of their 6-month active-duty requirements.

Also, on the grounds was the Coast Guard Institute, the institute developed and administered correspondence courses used by Coast Guardsmen to learn the skills needed to advance their career field. There were courses for every rating and each pay grade.

Student lived on the Training Station grounds, in rooms that accommodated six men comfortably. A force of 110 enlisted instructors was maintained at all times. These men were specially chosen for their jobs and met certain rigid qualifications.

My classmates were from all over, mostly from the east and west coast. One of my roommates was from Ely, Nevada. I was not the only person from a landlocked state. We were berthed in six-man rooms.

I do not have any clear memories about the classwork. We set in class all day listening to lectures, completing practical problems, taking written test, or doing typing exercises. In the evening we had homework to be completed before the next day.

We did not have to march to classes and meals like boot camp. When we were not in class, we were free to do as we please. There were no classes after 5 p.m. so we were free to roam the grounds and go to the Post Exchange (PX i.e., general store). During the week we were restricted to base. Since the Station was on the coast, I spent a lot of time sitting and listening to the waves breaking on the rocks that lined the shore. There was no beach.

On the weekend's liberty was granted so we could go into Groton, New London, and the surrounding area. I enjoyed looking at the hardwood trees, the rolling green meadows with the stone fences between fields. One weekend I went to Mystic Seaport near the Rhode Island state line. The seaport was a recreation of a whaling port. It was an entertainment complex. There were replicas of various ships including a whaling ship. The building rare replicas of what you find in a whaling port. It was just one big museum.

One of my memories was about a three-day holiday

weekend. One of my classmates owned a car and was from the Norfolk/Portsmouth area. Two classmates and I hitched a ride with him back to Portsmouth. I spent time with Linda Cherry and the Bland family. It was a busy weekend, and I burned the candle at both ends. On Tuesday, when I got back to base, I was scheduled for a dental appointment. After I received the Novocain, I was left alone for the medicine to take effect. The dentist chair was so comfortable that I went sound asleep for a few minutes. When I woke up everyone was running around trying to find out what they had done wrong. Me, I was just tired.

I graduated at the end of the 12-week class, and I was designated a seaman/yeoman striker (SNYN}. When I got my transfer papers, I was transferred back to the Fifth Coast Guard District in Portsmouth, VA. It was like going back home since this was where I was stationed before going to school.

CHAPTER 5

GROUP NORFOLK

After graduating from Yeoman School, I was transferred back to the Fifth CG District, Portsmouth, VA. I reported to the District Office in late October 1960. There I was assigned to CG Group, Norfolk, VA, just across the Elisabeth River from the District Office. This was the same base here the CGC *Chincoteague* moored.

The Group provided administrative and logistic support for the small boat stations and small cutters assigned to the Group. Group Norfolk's area of responsibility was from the outer banks of North Carolina north to Chincoteague Island in Maryland and Thomas Point Lighthouse in the Chesapeake Bay. As a Yeoman striker I would be working in the Personnel Office. Duties included entries into personal files, i.e., promotions, leave papers, address & dependent changes, etc. Also, I would type letters for the Chief Yeoman and the Executive Officer. On the 16th of January 1961 I had the "time in grade" and was advanced to Yeoman Third Class.

I do not remember much about living conditions at Group Norfolk. There must have been living quarters on base since I did not live off base. I did continue to visit Linda Cherry in Portsmouth, VA in my off-duty hours. Linda and I were not dating currently. I just hung out with her and her friends. I considered her family my home away from home.

I did not own a car, so I had to walk and ride a bus. To get to Linda's home I would catch a bus to downtown Norfolk. There I would transfer to a second bus to go thru a tunnel to downtown Portsmouth, VA. Then I would catch a third bus to ride out to the suburbs near where she lived. Last part of the trips I walked eight or nine blocks, through what was considered a bad (poor) part of town then several blocks of a nicer neighborhood. I could have bypassed the poor neighborhood, but it was much farther to travel and no bus. To get back to the base it was the same trip in reverse order.

Since I worked in the Group personnel office, I learned in early April that the yeoman billet on the USCGC *Narcissus* was going to be vacant. I ask for the job and on April 15, 1961. I was transferred to the *Narcissus*. I had joined the Coast Guard to be aboard ships, so this would be my second chance for sea duty. Also, I would be my own boss, answering only to the CO.

The USCGC *Narcissus* (WAGL-238) was a subunit of Group Norfolk. She handled inland buoys in the rivers and ship channels in southern Chesapeake Bay. The CGC *Narcissus* was 122' long, 28' beam with a draft of 8'. She was designed for light ice breaking if necessary. The captain (CO) was a W-4 Warrant Boatswain officer. The executive officer (XO) was a 1st Class Boatswain Mate. The engine room crew was headed by a 1st Class Engineman. There was a crew of about 17 enlisted men of various ratings. One of the billets was for a third-class yeoman.

My main job was to be the secretary for the ship. I shared an office with the CO, but he was gone most of the time. I had to type the CO's letters, fill out personnel reports, type leave papers, type daily duty roster, post corrections to official manuals, and of course filling. Typing letters was one of the things I disliked most. I was prone to making typing errors and my spelling was not the best. Most letters were 3 copies with carbon paper. When you make a mistake, it was a huge effort to correct, or maybe type over. I could not find my own errors immediately after typing. The next day I would look at the file copy and the error would jump right out at me. We did not have word processors then so if you made a mistake you had to type it over or use white out. Word processing on the computer is so much better.

There was not a storekeeper billet on the ship, so I had to do that job also. The job consisted mostly of ordering supplies for the deck force and the engineering department. The cook did all his own ordering. Ordering consisted mostly of typing up list that included a description, item number and quantity needed. On one occasion the 1st Class Boatswain ordered 210 feet of buoyant trail line. A couple of weeks later when two semi-trucks pulled up to the dock with 210 diesel engine alignment tools, I knew I was in trouble. Either the Boatswain had given me the wrong part number, or I had typed it incorrectly. Fortunately, the CO took care of the problem for me. I never did know where the alignment tools went.

When the ship's crew was at mooring stations for getting underway or docking, my duty station was telephone talker on the bridge. The telephone was a sound powered phone system used when not tied to the dock. The captain would give me instructions to pass to mooring station. I would get messages back from the mooring stations or engine room and pass the information to the captain. After we secured from mooring stations I would stay on the bridge and watch the sights while we sailed out of the harbor.

The job of the Narcissus was to maintain the buoys on the lower half of the Baltimore ship channel. This included small harbors like Crisfield, MD and the York, Rappahannock, and Potomac rivers. When we got underway on Monday to work buoys, we would normally dock on Monday night in Crisfield, MD. Sometimes we would be back in Crisfield on other nights, but a most of the time we would anchor out. We always anchored on the last night before returning home. The last night we was poker night. At the end of the scheduled work the ship would return to the dock in Norfolk on Thursday or Friday.

When the CGC *Narcissus* was moored at the dock we had two umbilical cords. One was for electricity and the other was the telephone. The official phone was in the CO's (my) office and a second telephone on the mess deck (dining room). The mess deck phone was for unofficial personal calls after working hours. Of course, the phones did not work when the mooring lines were cast off and the ship was underway. There was a radio on the bridge for communication when the *Narcissus* was at sea. A favorite prank was to wait until we were out in the ship channel, and then announce, over the loudspeaker, that a new seaman had a telephone call on the mess deck. He would go running to the mess deck and try to answer the phone. Of course, the new man would get a lot of ribbing after he discovered that the phone did not work when we were at sea.

One of my jobs as yeoman was to make corrections to various policy manuals, i.e., Aids-To-Navigation (AtoN) Manuel, Personnel Manuel, Storekeepers Manuel, etc. Making corrections meant removing pages and inserting new updated policy pages. One day while correcting the AtoN Manual I read one policy that caught my attention. Two days later I was still on the bridge after standing down from mooring stations. The Captain, a W-4 Warrant Boatswain, was talking to the 1st Class Boatswain about the policy I had just read. I spoke up and said, "Captain that's not right, they just changed the policy." The captain said in no uncertain terms that he had been in the service for 30 years and knew what the policy was. I went down to the office, got the AtoN Manual and took it up to the bridge to show him the change. I wanted to be sure that he knew about the new policy change. He read the new section, read it a second time, and said "that's not right". He then tore the page out of the book, wadded it up, and through it out the window. I took the manual and left the bridge. I stayed clear of the CO for a couple of day. I guess I embarrassed him in front of other people. Nobody ever accused me of being diplomatic.

As I stated earlier, the first night of the work week the ship would moor in Crisfield, MD. Crisfield was a small fishing village on the east side of Chesapeake Bay. There was not a lot to do there at that time. Most of the entertainment consisted of several small bars. I did not drink so I would just wander around and look at the scenery.

While moored at Crisfield the ship was on 30-minute standby for SAR calls. If we received a SAR call to get underway word was sent out to the bars and business for the crew to return to ship. One time we received a SAR call while I was at the far side of town and did not get the word until late. It was a sinking feeling when I walked back to the dock in time to see the ship sailing out the channel. Fortunately, a 40' patrol boat from the local CG Small Boat Station took me back to the ship.

During my off time aboard ship, I continued work on my education. I completed the correspondence course for YN2 on September 29, 1961, with high marks. With the completion of that course and the required time in grade I was promoted to YN2 on November 16, 1961.

Shortly after joining the *Narcissus*, Linda Cherry and I started going steady. Finely I ask Linda to marry me, and we sat a wedding date. None of my family was able to come the wedding. My dad did not feel like driving, so my older brother, Otis, was going to take off work and bring my mother. At the last minute he was not able to get off work, but no one called to let me know. On the morning of the wedding, I was at Linda's house getting ready. All morning I paced the front yard waiting for my mother and brother to show up and wondering where they were.

Linda and I were married on November 11, 1961, at a Baptist Church in Portsmouth, VA. I took 10 days leave so we could honeymoon in Richmond, VA. On our return we rented an apartment in Portsmouth, VA. This was across the Elizabeth River from where the *Narcissus* moored in Norfolk, VA. I still did not own a car, so I rode a bicycle to work. With the heavy traffic and many stop lights, I could get to work just as fast on a bike as I could have by auto.

The billet on the CGC *Narcissus* was for a YN3 and I was now a YN2. On May 24, 1962, I received orders transferring me back to the Personnel Office at CG Group Norfolk. That was just a walk down the dock.

As YN2 and with more experience, my new job was to process temporary duty orders (TDY) for personnel in the outlying small boat units. When a Guardsman went on leave, got sick or injured or left for training, personnel had to be transferred from one station to another to fill vacancies. That work could get hectic at times. It was like working a big jig saw puzzle.

In the Administrative building, where I worked, there was a large conference room. Once a month the officers from the base and the Fifth District Office, across the river in Portsmouth, would get together for a social hour and dinner. During the social hour a cash bar served mixed drinks. Usually, one of the stewards from the wardroom would act as bartender. On one occasion the regular bartender was not available. The Mess Officer came down to the personnel office and grabbed me. He said he needed me to be the bartender. I told him I knew nothing about mixing drinks. He said not to worry; he would show me what to do. It turned out that most of the drinks were simple drinks like rum and coke, scotch on the rocks, bourbon and water, etc. After that first time I tended bar on several occasions. It was not a bad job. I even earned some tips.

My Father died in June 1962. I was granted emergency leave to go to the funeral. My finances were not in good shape, and I was trying to figure out how I could pay for the trip home. The Red Cross gave me a grant to cover the cost of a plane ticket for me only. They would not pay for Linda. This really made me angry because no one in my family had met my wife. Linda was pregnant with our first child, and I desperately wanted her to meet my mother. In the end, I managed to come up with the additional funds for a plane ticket for Linda. I don't remember how I got the money, probably a loan. At the funeral I did not show feeling one way or the other. It was that night, in a motel room, with Linda in my arms that I broke down and cried. After a couple of days Linda and I traveled back to Portsmouth, VA.

On August 24, 1962, my first daughter, Sharon A. Beaty was born at the Norfolk Naval Hospital in Portsmouth, VA. Linda, Sharon, and I continued to live in the small apartment on High Street in Portsmouth VA. It was single family home had been converted into two apartments. Linda & I had the downstairs apartment. The second was occupied by a young Navy seaman and his wife.

In October 1962, the Cuban Missile Crisis occurred. All military and Coast Guard units went on DEVCON 3 (Defense Condition-3). That status meant that the US was not at war, but all units were to prepare for war. At Group Norfolk we were to secure the base perimeter and guard against unwanted people trying to gain access to the base. The enlisted men were assigned to sentry duty. They were issued M1 rifles and ammunition and posted to walk the boundary fence. About four days in, when things had started to calm down, one of the men fired his weapon by accident. The Base CO took all the ammunition away, but the men still had to walk sentry duty, with rifles. Talk about a Barny Fife event!!

In the middle of 1963, I was getting restless and began to look for a new assignment. I think I was probably bored and looking for a little adventure. In August 1963 I received orders and was transfer to the USCGC *Sagebrush* (WLB-399) in San Juan, Puerto Rico.

CHAPTER 6

SAN JUAN, PR

I reported on board the USCGC *Sagebrush* (WLB-399 in San Juan, Puerto Rico, on August 31, 1963. This was what was considered an "accompanied" tour. That means that I was authorized to have my family live with me in Puerto Rico. Linda and I had much discussion of the pros and cons of moving to San Juan, PR. Because Sharon was just one year old and Linda was pregnant again, we decided to for her to stay in Portsmouth, VA. There she would be close to her mother until the baby was born.

I traveled to Puerto Rico by air via Miami, FL. I wore my uniform, since I was under orders, and carried everything, including some civilian clothes, in my sea bag.

The *Sagebrush* was a Class C (*Iris* class) seagoing buoy tender. Her job was to maintain floating and fixed aids-to-navigation (AtoN) in Puerto Rico, the U.S. Virgin Islands, and surrounding waters. In addition to her main duties, she performed law enforcement, Search-and-Rescue (SAR), drug and illegal alien interdiction patrols, and provided logistical services in her area of operations. She also made occasional "show the flag" visits to various independent and colonial islands around the Leeward Islands to foster international familiarity and cooperation in the region.

USCGC *Sagebrush* (WLB-399)

The *Sagebrush* moored at the USCG Base in downtown San Juan. This was also the location of USCG Group San Juan. I was the only yeoman on the ship. My job, just like the CGC *Narcissus*, was to handle official correspondence for the Captain and Executive Officer, maintain personnel records, correct official publications and of course file. When the ship went to mooring stations, or during drills, my station was telephone talker on the bridge. When the ship was underway, I would work in the ship's office. There was a Storekeeper assigned so I did not have to handle the ordering of supplies.

Old San Juan is a beautiful place to visit. I enjoyed looking at all the old Spanish architecture and the beautiful churches. It was interesting to walk the narrow streets with tourist all over the place.

Then there was Morro Castle, built at the entrance to San Juan harbor. We got to look at it every time we got underway.

When liberty was granted, I would go and explore San Juan. The first place to visit was old town with its Spanish colonial buildings. Of course, Castillo San Felipe del Morro (El Morro Castle), which guards the entrance to the harbor, was one of the first places I visited. To stand there and look out over the ocean was beautiful sight. The walls around Old San Juan extended out from the Castle along the coast to east around the old town. At the bottom of the walls, on a narrow strip of land, was slum town. That was a large group of huts built from plywood, cardboard, timber, and tin. That was where the really poor people lived. Later I explored the newer section of San Juan. There was wide strip of upscale hotels stretching along the beach on the north coast. One of the hotels, The Coronado Hilton I think, stands out in my mind, because it had a beach front lounge with a low bar. Patrons sat in lounge chairs at the bar. You could sit at the bar, with a drink, a soda in my case, and listen to the waves roll in.

After a few months, I started going out to the bars at night with some of my shipmates. The crew seemed to like one bar. It was called La Cucaracha. That name is Spanish for The Cockroach. The bar was a little run down, but it was within walking distance of the ship. By this time, I had started to drink a few mixed drinks. I still did not drink beer. I would drink a rum and coke, then a straight coke, then repeat the sequence throughout the night. After one of these nights, I would lay in my bunk wide awake. I could not understand why I couldn't sleep. Years later I come to understand that it was the caffeine and sugar in the cokes that was the problem. I wasn't hung over the next morning, but I sure was tired from lack of sleep.

We were under way most weeks working buoys all around Puerto Rico and surrounding islands. Most of the trips were routine and one voyage was just like the next. There were a few that stood out in my memory.

One such cruse was a logistics run to refuel an unmanned lighthouse on Mona Island. Mona Island is kidney shaped about 7 miles long and 4 miles wide and is located about 41 miles west of Puerto Rico. The island is the largest of three in the strait between Puerto Rico and the Dominican Republic. There were 200 ft. cliffs all the way around the island. The lighthouse, on the northwest coast of the island, was there because at night, the island looked like low lying cloud on the horizon. In fact, one northbound ship had beached itself on the south side of the island and I saw the remains when we sailed around the island.

When we got to the island, the ship had to anchor on the north side. There was a small rundown dock, but it was too small to moor alongside. We were delivering diesel fuel. The ship offloaded 55 gal. drums over the side and into the water. The drums would float and were towed into the wharf by small boat. At the dock the drums were man handled onto the wharf and rolled up to the beach. I don't remember how the drums got from the beach to the lighthouse.

Between trips the small boat made to the ship and back with drums, there was a waiting period. While the dock crew was waiting, we got a chance to look around. There were marine iguanas all over the place. These were large lizards, some as big as 4 foot long. We were not in danger. The iguanas were afraid of us and would run in the other direction.

Near the wharf, the clefts were honey combed with caves. The rumor was that the caves went all the way from one side to the other. I walked into one cave as far as I could see. The cave went on and on, but without a light I was concerned about getting lost. Later years I often thought about going back to explore the caves.

Once you got to the top to the cliff the land was flat and covered with brush. There were still goats and hogs on the island. I did see a section of abandoned narrow gage railroad track. The old track was used to move supplies from the wharf to the Lighthouse. The rumor was that before World War I the Germans used to mine guano from bat droppings in the caves. The guano was used in manufacturing of fertilizer.

On another occasion the crew had to play "pack mule" for a civilian contractor. The contractor's job was to repair an unmanned light house on one of the islands. The light was high on a rugged hilltop. The supplies had been flown in by a helicopter. When the air crew dropped the lumber and bags of cement, they put them in the wrong place not clost to the job site. Our job was to manually move the materials up to the light location.

On the way back from that assignment, the Sagebrush anchored offshore of Vieques Island. Vieques is located east of Puerto Rico. At the time I was there the island was used a gunnery and bombing range by U.S. Navy. The captain decided that the crew had been working hard and needed some R&R (rest and recreation). He arranged for us to have a picnic on the white sandy beach. All afternoon we relaxed, swam and had a great cookout. The captain had brought a couple of cases of beer that trip. No beer for me, but I did enjoy snorkeling in the crystal-clear water. I cannot describe the sight of all the colorful fish swimming among the coral.

Saint Croix is an island in the Caribbean Sea, located southeast of Puerto Rico. It is one of the U.S. Virgin Islands. The island is about 82 sq. mi. in area and is 22 miles long and 7 miles wide. The CGC

Sagebrush would go to St. Croix at least once a year to maintain the buoys and more often if a buoy was reported off station.

The ship made the trip once while I was aboard. The ship would work AtoN during the day and moor at Frederiksted at night. The language is officially English. I found the people hard to understand because they talked so fast, and they had their own Danish Creole dialect. Before the island became an American territory, the island had been part of the Danish West Indies.

On one liberty I went ashore to one of the local nightspots. At night, with the dim lights, the place looked quite interesting. A couple of days later I saw the same bar during the day, boy what a dump.

One of the lights we had to service was on the top of a small island that was about 350 to 400 feet high. The climb was up a steep slope of about 45-degree angle. The work party, which I was part of, had to carry extra batteries and water to charge the batteries. Going up was a chore but coming down was just as bad. One man got to going too fast and couldn't stop. He ran straight into a large cactus plant. The corpsman spent the whole evening, using plyers/ to pull thorns out one by one.

The only SAR call that we had while I was aboard had to do with a freighter started to sink while in port. The freighter was moored near a small town on the south side of Puerto Rico. The ship was loading guano to haul to a fertilizer plant. The leaking saltwater mixing with bird poop was giving off hydrogen gas. The gas was building up in the hold and there was the potential for a spark to cause a large explosion. If this happened the town would be destroyed, and many people injured. The Sagebrush sailed around to the south side of the island and moored in the bay as far away from the freighter as we could get. We were there to tow the ship out to sea if the pressure in the holds could not be released. Finally, the Captain came up with a plan to take a small volunteer crew in a small boat, and go over and open the relief valves to let the gas escape. To do this we needed some brass wrenches, something not normally used. Normal steel and iron wrenches could potentially cause a spark when used on metal bolts. The Engineering Officer just happened to have the right wrenches. The Captain and boat crew went over, opened the valves, problem solved.

President John F. Kennedy was killed on November 22, 1963. That was a Friday and the CGC *Sagebrush* was steaming back into San Juan harbor after a week of working buoys. Since we were in the ship channel getting ready to moor, I was on the bridge as a telephone talker. The news was received over the radio. Everyone on the bridge was stunned.

It was lonely being away from Linda and Sharon. It was tough for Linda also, but she had family close by for support. We wrote letters back and forth and when I could afford it I would call. Long distance telephone calls were very expensive. No cell phones at that time. Time drug by slowly, but I had my work on the ship to keep me busy.

On December 6, 1963, my son, M. David, was born at the U.S. Naval Hospital in Portsmouth, VA. The ship was underway working buoys when the news was received over the radio. The Captain called me to the bridge to give me the news. I did not get much work done that day. The XO ask me if I wanted leave to travel back to the States. I told him no, that Linda and I had talked it over, and I wanted to wait so I could be home for Christmas. I was granted 10 days leave over the Christmas and New Year holiday. I traveled to Roosevelt Roads Naval Base on the eastern side of Puerto Rico. There I caught a space available flight on a C-130 aircraft going to Norfolk Naval Air Station. It was warm when I left Puerto Rico, so I traveled in dress whites. That was a mistake. In Norfolk Virginia it was bitter cold when I got off the plane. I thought I was going to freeze my butt off before I got home in Portsmouth.

When leave was over, way too short, I went back to the ship. A month later on February 2, 1964 I transferred to San Juan Group Office. This was on the base where the CGC *Sagebrush* moored. Once at the Group Office I qualified for off base housing, and I made arrangements for Linda, Sharon and David to join me.

A normal accompanied tour (serve with family) in Puerto Rico was two years. Since Linda did not travel with me originally, I had to agree to extend for a longer tour in Puerto Rico. No big deal, I enjoyed my time on the island.

When the family arrived, we were assigned enlisted housing in a navy housing complex about twenty miles from the CG Station. Officers were housed on an Army Base a short distance away. This subdivision was filled with duplex housing units, a small convenience store, laundry mat, move theater, and several small playgrounds. It was about 15 minutes to the main Naval Base. I did not have a car which was the case for most dependents. The Navy provided a bus to get to the Commissary and Post Exchange. The whole complex was surrounded with a tall chain link fence. With the gate and security guard at the entrance it felt like a prison. Then we found our why. About once a year, around election time, there would be riots in the streets. Puerto Rico is just an American territory not a state. The people are U.S. citizens but they do not have representation in Congress. They still don't. Sone people strongly wanted to be the 51st. state, but others strongly wanted things to stay as they were. So when it came time to vote for statehood things would get interesting.

It was tough for Linda at first. She had a one-year-old and a baby to take care of and no friends at first. I was out to sea Monday to Friday on most weeks. We did not have a car, so Linda had to ride the bus to the doctor's office or to buy food. Linda particularly did not like the 2-inch lizards that would crawl on the ceilings. And it would rain just about every day at four o'clock. You could just about set your watch by the rain. It would rain for about 15 minutes and then it would clear up. The rest of the day would be dry. The ladies would not bother taking the laundry off the line when it rained. They would wait and the clothes would dry before dark.

At Group San Juan I was assigned to the personnel office. I would be doing much the same work as I did at Group Norfolk. I continued to study my correspondence courses and completed my Yeoman First Class (YN1) course with 97%. I had time in grade for YN1, but at time advancement in the yeoman rating was closed for lack of openings. It looked like it would be several years before I could advance.

Word came down from Headquarters in Washington that there were openings for enlisted personal, second class or above, to apply for OCS (officer candidate school) as aviation cadets. Since I had originally wanted to be an officer, and advancement in my rate was closed, it sounded like a good idea and I applied. Learning to fly sounded like fun. Several weeks later I received orders to travel to Miami Florida to take the test and physical for aviation cadet. I arrived in Miami and on Monday morning I went to a downtown office building to take the written exams. The exams were very tough. During lunch I walk around downtown thinking that I had not done very well on the test. After lunch I was told that I had passed the test and was to proceed to the medical office for exams. The first medical exam was on the eyes. I passed with 2020 vision. On the next medical exams I met all the requirements, so I was thinking that I had a good chance of being accepted. Then the corpsman told me that there was one more eye exam. My eyes were dilated so the doctor could check the inside of my eyes. This time he found that I had stigmatism and that would disqualify me. I qualified for regular OCS but there were no openings at that time. I was really disappointed. For the second time I missed my chance to becoming an officer. I traveled back to San Juan on a navy flight in a very depressed mood. By the time I got home I had calmed down... Hey, I had a job that I enjoyed, and every now and then I could go sailing on a ship. What more could you ask.

Since I couldn't be an officer, I wanted to go back to sea. A yeoman position opened up on the USCGC *Aurora* (WPC-103) assigned to Group San Juan. On May 12, 1964 I received orders and was transferred to the *Aurora*.

The USCGC *Aurora* was a Thetis class 165' long patrol craft. She was 25' wide and had a draft of 10'. The cutter had twin screw with two six-cylinder diesel engines. This gave us a cursing speed of 11 knots and a max speed of 16 knots. SAR, marine law enforcement and drug interdiction were the primary mission of the Aurora.

CGC *Marion* sister ship of CGC *Aurora*

We would go periodic patrols around Puerto Rico. When in port the crew was on 2 hour and 30-minute SAR standby. Standby meant that the *Aurora* had to be underway within designated period from the time the message was received on board. This was a little hard to do at times. You had to stay home in case a call came in. There were no telephones in the housing units. There was one pay telephone booth outside one of crews home.

When a SAR call was received, the OOD (officer of the day) would have the quartermaster of the watch would call the pay phone first, and then the OOD would call the Captain and other officers. The person answering the pay phone would go and knock on the other crewmember's doors, go back get his gear, and we would all pile into a car and head to the ship. If the Captain, who lived farther from the ship than enlisted crew, got to the ship first and had minimum crew on board to operate the ship, would get underway and leave us behind. It is a sinking feeling to get to the dock and see the ship sailing out the harbor. This happened to us a couple of times. One of the times I got left behind was for a SAR case where a fishing boat had capsized. The Aurora was able to rescue the crew from the water.

The *Aurora* had a wooden picnic table on the fantail. In the evenings after work or off duty underway, we would sit at the table and socialize. The only problem was with the CO and the XO. The CO, a lieutenant commander, would come back and visit with the crew and complain about the XO. When he left the XO, a lieutenant, would come back and complain about the CO. That is something that should not be done. Bad blood between officers should not be aired in front of the enlisted men. This bickering was bad for moral.

Linda and I lived in a two-bedroom duplex. The other side of the duplex was one bedroom. After a couple of months Linda started to make friends with other coast guard and navy wives. For entertainment we would go to the movies at the theater in the complex. We would play cards with friends on Friday nights.

To go out on the town we would go to the enlisted men's club at the Army base about 10 minutes away. There we could get a good meal, then go to the lounge for music and of course booze. The theme song for the club was "I want to go Home." There were two groups of enlisted men assigned to Puerto Rico. One faction liked the customs and culture, the architecture and tried to learn the language. While English was the official language many of the locals spoke a Spanish dialect. This group enjoyed themselves and had a good tour of duty. Some even married Puerto Rican women. The second group didn't like the people, didn't like the culture, and didn't like the language. These were the ones that would go to the club and cry in their beer and sing "I want to go home" several times a night. I got tired of listening to them after a while.

When David was about 6 months old the family went to one of the white sandy beaches nearby. Sharon enjoyed herself but David would have nothing to do with the ocean. If we got him near the waves he would scream in terror. We really enjoyed the outing if we kept David away from the water.

Along about November I noticed that Linda was getting more and more depressed. She was not adjusting well to being away from the life she was accustomed to. Finally in December she had a small nervous breakdown. The Doctor recommended she go back to the United States. I arranged for an emergency transfer, on December 30, 1964, I took my family and returned to Portsmouth, Virginia.

CHAPTER 7

THE RESERVE OFFICE

I took 10 days leave as part of my transfer back to the States. During this time, I moved my family to Portsmouth, Virginia to be near Linda's family. We found a two-bedroom duplex not too far from the office where I would be working. The other half of the duplex was occupied by a single lady just a couple of years older than Linda. She and Linda became good friends. I made an appointment with a doctor at the Portsmouth Naval Hospital, to help Linda with her depression. With all that taken care of, I was ready to report back to work at the end of my leave.

I reported to the Fifth Coast Guard District Office in Portsmouth, VA on January 10th, 1965. There I was assigned to work in the District Reserve Office. This office provided personnel and administrative assistance to the Coast Guard Reserve units in Virginia, West Virginia, and North Carolina. The office consisted of 5 officers, 8 enlisted yeomen and 5 civilian personnel. I still did not own a car, so I took a city bus to work.

Since reservist drilled only one weekend a month with two weeks active duty each summer there were a lot of policy differences from regular Coast Guardsmen. My first job was to learn the different regulations. Other than new policies, the work was much the same as work aboard ship. Just a lot of paperwork and entries in personnel files.

One of the more interesting parts of the work was learning about early version of a computer. At that time, they were called EAM (electronic counting machines). The process worked by first having personnel data entered onto a special 80 space report. This report would include information such a name, rank, Guard unit, training, etc. This report was sent to a key punch operator to type (think: punch) the data onto an 80-space punch card. This card was about 4 inches by 8 ½ inches in size. A second key punch operator would enter the same data as a cross check. If both operators agreed, the card was sent on to be filed. When a report was need, such as how many First-Class Boatswain Mates there were in the district reserve units, the cards were pulled from file and sent to be processed. Information was obtained by running large bunches of punch cards through a sorting machine. This machine would select the cards needed by reading the holes punched in the card. The brain of the sorting machine was a board that had 80 holes down and 80 rows across. These first rows of holes down were connected by short wires to the holes going across. This would sort the cards according to the data needed. The selected cards would then be read by a machine that would print out the report needed. This was a much faster method than going through the personnel files by hand.

I got along well with the enlisted men I worked with. Every now and then those that were married would get together for a BBQ or some other party. Just before Christmas 1965 Linda and I had a party at our house. It was a Christmas tree decorating party. Our friends came over and we made colored paper chains, strung popcorn, cut out snowflakes, etc. The ladies made and decorated homemade cookies. There was a lot of laughter and just good old fun. In fact, we had so much fun we held a New Year's party the next week. That was a bring your own bottle and we supplied the snacks. We undecorated the Christmas tree, threw it out the front yard, and moved the furniture up against the wall. Then we had food, fun, music and dancing until midnight. One of the men got plastered so we took his keys away and would not let him drive home. He was so drunk that he could not remember where he left his car the next day. His wife thanked us for not letting him drive.

In the summer of 1965, I planned a trip to Pawnee, OK. I had been married for four years, had two children, but no one in my family had met my children. I decided that it was time to correct the situation.

At this point I still did not own an automobile. I went to a used car lot to purchase an inexpensive car. I had not owned a car as a teenager. I either hitch hiked or borrowed my dad's old GMC pickup. I purchased a car that looked like it would make the trip, and I could afford. The car came with two bad tires on the front. With the purchase of two new tires, I was ready to go.

Linda and I packed the bags, loaded the children in the car, and we were on the way. This would be my first drive across country. Since Pawnee was on U.S. Highway 64, I decided to drop south to pick up U.S. 64 in North Carolina and follow it all the way home.

There were no interstate highways at that time. Everything was going well until we got to the Appalachian Mountains in western North Carolina. That road was so crocked that you could see your taillights when going round a hair pen curve, well almost. Linda got so car sick that I had to stop in Tennessee and see a doctor. He gave her some motion sickness pills and sent us on our way.

We had a great time in Oklahoma. It was a busy few day running around getting reacquainted with the family. Everyone wanted to oooh and aaah over the children. I had not seen my younger sister and brother in five years. My older brother was back from the army. He had returned with a young wife from Berlin, Germany.

In no time at all, it was time for the return trip back to Virginia. I planned to take a more direct route that was a few miles shorter. Being young and foolish I was going to drive the trip nonstop. I got as far as the Blue Ridge Mountains in Virginia before I got so tired that I had to get some rest. Linda had not driven on a long trip before and did not want to drive now. I stopped and picked up a Navy sailor that was hitch hiking back to Norfolk, VA. I let him drive while I rested. Going down the last hill out of the mountains, one of the front tires blew. It was one of the new tires that I had purchased before the trip. The tire was worn down to the threads on one edge. Unknown to me the front end was out of alignment. That was why the front tires were bad when I bought the car. After changing the tire, we were able to creep on in to Norfolk.

The next weekend I had someone look at the Car. The problem was that the front ball joint on the driver's side was bad. Being young, dumb and short on good sence, I decided that I would fix the problem myself. I bought new ball joint parts, some tools and started to work. After a couple of days, I realized that replacing a ball joint was something that I could not do myself. Later I learned that even mechanics a hard time with that type of repair. That was when I decided to sell the car for junk. Then I went out and bought myself a new Volkswagen Bug.

Part of the job was to make administrative inspections of Coast Guard Reserve Units. I was the designated driver on one of these inspection trips. There were two officers, one a Commander, a Lieutenant, the Chief Yeoman and me. The officers meet with the reserve unit officers while the chief and I inspected files and personnel records. On the way back home the Commander was riding up front while I drove. As we came up on a country restaurant the Commander said, "you can stop for a cup of coffee if you want". I said I don't drink coffee and keep on driving. The YNC tapped me on the shoulder and said the Commander wants a cup of coffee. I stopped at the next location. That's when I learned that that an officer's suggestion is a polite order.

The district office was in a tall office building right on the Elizabeth River waterfront. Between us and the river was an empty pier where the warehouse had been torn down. The pier was paved and used as a parking lot for employees. The pavement was about 15 to 20 feet above normal water level. One day we had an extreme high tide because of the phase of the moon. That day there was also a strong rainy northeaster storm with a high storm surge. The water level came up to the window level of cars parked on the pier. That was the worst storm I had seen. A lot of downtown Portsmouth was flooded.

In late 1965 there was a call for enlisted personnel E2 or above, all ratings, to apply for Officer Candidate School (OCS).

Since my promotion to YN1 was still closed with no openings in sight, I decided to apply. Here was my third chance to become and officer. I had already passed the written test required, back in Miami. The physical was no problem this time. The last thing needed was an interview board consisting of three officers. The president of the board was from my office and had been my division officer when I was on the USCGC *Chincoteague*. His name was John D. O'Malley. His current rank was LCDR. The interview lasted for about 30 minutes, and then I was excused. They did not let me know what their recommendation was. I went back to work and had to wait to find out what the outcome would be. A couple of weeks later I was notified that I was accepted for OCS school and I would be assigned the next school. The Coast Guard only ran two OCS classes a year.

In February 1966 I received orders to report to the Commanding Officer, Coast Guard Reserve Training Center in Yorktown, Virginia for instruction as an Officer Cadet. Yorktown was about 2 hours north of Portsmouth, VA and located on the York River. The first two months I would be restricted to the base, so Linda decided stay in our home in Portsmouth.

CHAPTER 8

OFFICER CANDIDATE SCHOOL

I reported to the Reserve Training Center in February 1966. I was not sure what to expect but I was ready for the next phase of my career. The Training Center was a beautiful 500-acre campus right on the banks of the York River. It was just a short distance southeast of the site of the last battle of the Revolutionary War.

The Officer Candidate School program (OCS) is a highly specialized, 17-week course of instruction. The academic curriculum covered operational Coast Guard missions, leadership, nautical science, navigation, law enforcement, and fundamental military training. Upon graduation junior officers could expect assignments in one of three areas: duty aboard ship, marine safety and civilian vessel inspection, or response management, i.e., search & rescue, law enforcement, pollution investigation and others.

Upon reporting on board, after my orders were processed, I was turned over to the OCS staff. When all the officer applicants had reported in there were about 64 of us. The class consisted of eight enlisted men from the Coast Guard, and the rest were reservists that were college graduates. The class was divided into four platoons. I was assigned to Alpha platoon. The platoon would march to class, eat, perform close order drill, attend class, and do everything else as a group.

We were assigned quarters in wooden two-story barracks building left over from World War II. Alpha platoon was on the ground floor in one of the two barracks. We would live two men to a room for the rest of our time at OCS. My roommate was a reservist from St. Louis, MO.

The first week consisted of getting uniforms, bedding, and books issued. After storing our gear in our rooms, we were marched off to get haircuts. Each platoon had a DI (drill instructor) which was a LTJG (lieutenant junior grade with one silver bar on his collar).

The Drill Instructor's job was to teach us social etiquette, how to wear our uniforms properly, how to keep our rooms ship shape, and how to move and work as a team. In other words, be our nursemaid while we were at the Training Center. Once we had stored our gear and got our rooms organized, the next order of business was to teach us the basics of military drill. Having been through the boot camp, the enlisted cadets had an easier time with the drilling. We were able to give pointers to our college brothers. It had been over six years since I had been to boot camp, so I could use some refresher training. The DI would conduct room inspection from time to time to ensure that we kept our rooms organized.

One of the first things the DI taught us was how to form up outside the barracks. On the command "Fall In" we would rush outside and gather into platoon formation. We learned to stand at "Attention" which was standing straight, eyes forward, chest out, knees straight but not locked, feet together. We also learned Parade Rest which was a modified position of attention in which the feet are moved to shoulder width and the hands are clasp in the small of the back. Some of the other commands we would quickly learn were at ease, rest, fallout, and dismissed. We would also learn to "Dress Right", i.e., look to the right, straighten the column, and ensure arm length space between men. The DI spent a lot of time yelling in our faces, especially when we did something wrong.

After learning to form up, we spent a lot of time marching (called close order drill) to and from the chow hall and everywhere else we had to go. That first week we spent a lot of time on the drill field practicing close order formations. The drill field was a large open area just behind the barracks. Military drill is memorizing certain actions through repetition until the actions are instinctive. Complex actions are broken down into simpler steps which can be practiced separately so when the individual steps are put together the desired results are achieved. Once we learned the basics of close order drill, we were issued rifles. Then we drilled with a rifle (called manual of arms) until we got the routine down. Some people, when they made mistakes, did some "high port" around the drill field just like boot camp.

After the first month, one of the platoon members was designated as platoon leader. It was his job to march the platoon from location to location. He would also oversee the drilling of the platoon on the grinder. The DI would still supervise the drill practice. But this would take some of the pressure of the DI. Each week the position of platoon leader would change so everyone received a chance to be in charge.

About midway through the course the OCS Instructors started selecting one person to be Company Commander. I think the person selected was based on grades and recommendations by the four Drill Instructors. The Company Commander was in charge of all four platoons when we practiced marching as a company. He was also in charge when we had inspection formations each Saturday morning. The Company Commander and Platoon Commanders were issued swords to carry when we were marching under arms (carrying rifles).

After a week of drilling, it was time to get serious about our studies. Our classes were divided into four general areas: Navigation, Seamanship, CIC and Administration. The DI was also an instructor in one of the many classes we had to take.

Navigation consisted mainly of classes on piloting and dead reckoning, use of charts and tide tables and celestial navigation. There were a lot of problems to be solved in class and homework back at the barracks.

Seamanship covered nautical Rules of the Road, shipboard organization, basic seamanship, ship handling, damage control and aids to navigation.

In the CIC section we learned the use of maritime radio, radar, and plotting the course of other ships. This section covered search and rescue and how to conduct search patterns to locate someone or something in the water.

The Administration portion of the course covered wide range of information that a new junior officer would need. Subjects included Coast Guard history, Coast Guard missions, Coast Guard organization, military justice, publications and directives, maritime law enforcement, civil rights, and leadership.

In the second half of the course the class went through some team building and leadership exercises. The platoon was divided into five- or six-man teams and each team would be given a problem to solve. One member would be designated leader and he was to direct the group in solving the exercise. There were enough exercises, so everyone had a chance to be team leader. I do not remember how the problems worked, but I do remember many 55-gallon barrels and a lot of planks. One of the exercises was launching and manning a pulling boat.

I was the team leader on the rowing exercise. Everything went well until we reached our goal and started back to the dock. The instructor hollered and suggested that I had someone put in the boat plug before the boat sank. Looking down I saw the boat slowly filling with water.

Every Saturday morning, we would fall out and form up for uniform inspection. The OCS School's Commanding Officer or his assistant would inspect the troops checking to see if the uniforms were worn correctly, shoes were spit shined, hair cut to proper length, and anything else they could find. After falling out from inspection the DIs would conduct "white glove" inspections of the rooms. Anyone found lacking in either inspection would be issued demerits. Demerits could be worked off by extra drilling, cleaning latrines or other odd jobs around the barracks.

Wearing a proper uniform and accessories was always required. One of the rules was that we had to wear a hat anytime we were outside the building. If we were in dress uniform, we had to wear the peaked hat. During the last month we were given passes and allowed to go off base on the weekend. One of the enlisted cadets was six foot 3 inches tall. He had a Volkswagen bug to drive when he went on a weekend pass. Since he had to wear the peaked hat, it was difficult for him to get in the car. His VW bug had a sunroof, if it was not raining, he would open the sunroof, and you would see him drive by with the top of the hat sticking out above the top of the car.

We were not allowed to smoke inside the buildings. On one occasion while we were lined to go into the mess hall, one of the cadets lit a cigarette. When it came his time to go inside, he put the cigarette out and saved it in his shirt pocket. The cigarette was not completely out and burned a hole in his shirt. We knew his major in college was Fire Protection Engineering. He got a lot of ribbing about setting himself on fire.

Close to the end of school an officer from the Personnel Office in Washington, D.C. came down to talk to us about the officer assignment process and career path assignment. All cadets were given a form to fill out indicating our desire for the type of duty we would go to upon graduation. You were given three choices of type of duty or part of the U.S. you would like to be assigned. I sure grades were a big factor on where your first tour of duty would be.

After the last exam was taken, we began to make preparations for our graduation ceremony. A Rear Admiral would be down from Headquarters in Washington, D.C. He would inspect the company and then give a speech at our graduation.

The final grades were posted and then a list of duty assignments was handed out. I found out that I was going to the USCGC *Gentian* (WLB-290) home port, Galveston, TX. This suited me just fine. I wanted shipboard duty. I had served on two buoy tenders and had some idea what the work would be like. As far as grades went, I found out that I was number three in the class. I had worked hard at my studies and was proud of my class standing.

Final paperwork was completed, orders were issued, uniforms were packed, and I was ready for the next phase of my Coast Guard career.

Formal inspection was held on Saturday morning by the Rear Admiral. The graduation ceremony was at 1 p.m. Guests were encouraged to attend, and Linda came up from Portsmouth, VA. to help me celebrate.

The Officer Candidates and their guest gathered in the Base auditorium. The Commanding Officer of the school gave a short talk. Awards were handed out by the various departments. Next came the presentation for the outstanding Officer Candidate for our Class. The trophy for the outstanding Cadet was a ceremonial officer's sword. We all waited for the name of the person to receive this award. I was speechless when my name was called. I went up on the stage to receive the sword. Next the Admiral gave the speech, diplomas were awarded and we were free to go.

We were now Ensigns (O-1) in the U.S Coast Guard and entitled to receive salutes from the enlisted men. Chief Petty officers and 1st Class petty officers that had helped in our training were outside the auditorium. The custom was that the first enlisted man that saluted a new officer should be given a dollar bill. That was one dollar that I was thrilled to give away.

Linda and I went back home to plan to move to Galveston. I was eligible to have the government pay to move my furniture. The movers came, packed up our belongings and hauled them away. Linda and I loaded the kids and our bags in the car. We said goodbye to our friends and Linda's family, then we were on our way to new adventure.

CHAPTER 9

USCGC *GENTIAN* (WLB-290)

Unlike other moves we had made, Linda the children and I decided to travel by car. Being young, foolish, and short on cash, we planned to drive as far as possible before stopping for the night. Galveston was halfway across country but according to the atlas if would be less than a 24-hour drive. We were west of New Orleans, but still in Louisiana, when I decided to stop for the night. The motel was older but looked in good shape. I was surprised when we got to the room. There were two front doors, like an air lock. The next morning, I found out why. I went outside to put the luggage in the car. The misquotes swarmed all over me. It was like a cloud bank. The air lock was to try to keep misquotes out. I grabbed the kids and Linda, jumped in the car and left just as fast as we could. The second day we finished the trip to Galveston and reported for duty.

First item of business was to locate housing for my family. At the Group Galveston Housing Office, I was assigned quarters at the officer's housing complex at Fort Crockett. Fort Crockett was an old Army base that had provided defense for the Galveston harbor. During WWII the defensives had been upgraded with the addition of long-range artillery. It was also a German POW camp during the war. The Army had turned the base over to other government agencies after the war.

The officer's housing was group of two story, stone duplex buildings. The complex was located right on Seawall Boulevard. The only thing between my house and the Gulf of Mexico was a seawall and a four-lane street. The houses were so close to the water that when there was a storm, the waves would break on the seawall and spray would come all the way to the house. I was glad that the vehicle parking was at the back of the house.

The house I was assigned was clean, had large rooms, but there was no furniture. Our furniture was not due to arrive for another week. In fact, it was about five weeks before it finally showed up. The wives of the other officers took Linda in hand and got the situation solved. They went back to the Housing Office and arranged for some basic loaner furniture. We made do with this until our furniture arrived. Linda was as new to this officer life as I was. The other wives were big help to her.

Now that my family was settled in, it was time for me to go back to work. I reported on board the USCGC *Gentian* (WLB-290). One of my classmates was reporting at the same time. The CGC *Gentian* was a 180 ft., A-class seagoing buoy tender. She had been commissioned back in November 1942 which made almost as old as I was. She was 37 ft. wide, with a draft of 12 ft. The propulsion system was a single screw with two diesel electric motors. That would give us a cruising speed of 11 knots (13 mph). The crew consisted of 4 officers, 2 warrants and 42 enlisted.

Because I had received good grades in navigation studies at OCS, I was given the job as Navigator and Division Officer for the Operations Division. Included in the Operations Division was the quartermasters, radio operator, radar man and electronics repairman. My classmate and I, as the two new Ensigns (O-1), divided up the minor shipboard duties usually assigned to the junior officers.

Shipboard living as an officer was different than when I was enlisted. As enlisted, there would be fifteen to twenty men to a compartment. Junior officers were berthed two people to a cabin. Of course, the officers shared a bathroom and shower (called head). The officers had their own officer's mess or wardroom. The president of the officer's mess was the Executive Officer. The Captain took meals in his own cabin, but often he was invited down to the wardroom.

The CGC *Gentian's* area of operation was from the Galveston ship channel east to and including the mouth of the Mississippi River and all the ocean buoys in between. Galveston harbor was the entrance to the Huston ship channel, but the channel markings for the Huston channel were maintained by river buoy tinder. The large entrance channel buoys had to be serviced once a year by the Gentian.

Working buoys on CGC *Gentian* (WLB-290)

Working a buoy included hoisting the buoy on deck, checking the sinker (2000 lb. concrete block), and inspecting the mooring chain. While on deck the marine growth would be scraped off, new paint applied, batteries changed, and light bulbs inspected.

Placing the buoy back in the water was a critical revolution. The sinker is lowered over the side and secured by a chock; the chain is flacked out on deck, while the buoy is hoisted over the side ready to release. On the bridge the quartermaster and his helpers would take bearings on three separate items located on a chart. The Captain or OOD (Officer of the Deck) slowly maneuvers the ship into position. Meanwhile the navigator is plotting three bearings on a chart. When the three bearings come together on a single point, the plotter yells "on station," the captain yells down to the buoy deck "let go". The chock is opened, the sinker drops, chain rattles across the deck and the buoy is set. The chain really whips out fast, so the deck crew must take care to stay out of the way. The ship maneuvers away from the buoy then proceeds to the next buoy. This process is repeated over and over again, all day long.

Not all the work was doing buoy maintenance work. Quiet often we would get a call that a buoy was off station, i.e., not in its charted position. A lot of the time it would be a tug and barge that would get too close to the buoy and pull it off station. Since ships use the buoys to show them where the dredged channel is located, it is important that buoys stay on their charted station. A buoy off station could cause a ship to run aground. When a "buoy off station" call came in we would stop what we were doing and proceed to the new location. If the *Gentian* was in port for the weekend, but "on standby" the crew would be called back to the ship, and we would get underway to take care of the problem.

If we were working buoys in the same location two or three days in a row the Gentian would anchor offshore for the night. A lot of the time we would cruse from one location to another overnight so we would be ready to work buoys first thing in the morning. At other times it would be too fogy, or the wind and waves would be too strong to work buoys. It was always a guess what the next day would bring.

One of the first order of business was to be trained and learn to stand seagoing watches as OOD. We had to learn the Eighth Coast Guard District chain of command, shipboard routine; the ship's handling characteristics, radio call signs, Captain's standing orders and much more. As new Ensigns my classmate and I would stand watch with another officer until we became qualified. As OOD trainees we were responsible for the safety of the ship while under way. This included keeping an eye out for other ships or objects; seeing that the helmsman steered a straight course; overseeing the quartermaster; keeping the ship's logbook and everything else that needed to be done.

One of the responsibilities of the Navigator was to send out a message when we sailed telling the District Office when we departed and what area we would be working. If the ship was going to be away from the dock for several days, I would send a message at 8 a.m. and 8 p.m. with our location. After the work was done and it was time to head back to the dock, we would send a message telling the District our ETA (estimated time of arrival). The reason for these messages was to let the District know our location in cast here was a serious accident or collusion.

The CGC *Gentian* docked at a pier near downtown Galveston. Leaving harbor, we had to navigate around incoming cargo ships, sail boats and pleasure craft, and the ferry that ran across the channel going from Galveston to the Bolivar peninsula. Because of this marine traffic we were always 10 to 15 minutes late making our ETA. It became a challenge to see how accurate my ETA would be. After studding these arrivals for a few months, I started calculating our ETA and adding 10 minutes to the time. After that we always made our message ETA within 3minutes on either side. One evening the Captain read the ETA message before it was sent out. He had calculated our arrival time in his head and ask why my time was different. I told him about the 10-minute dead time that I added. He told me to never add the 10 minutes again. Of course, I complied, but we never made our ETA again.

The Gulf of Mexico between Galveston and the mouth of the Mississippi River was dotted with offshore oil rigs. These rigs were stationary and were plotted on the charts that we used for navigation. Underway the bridge crew would take bearings on the rigs and plot our position. This type of navigation, called dead reckoning, was what we used in coastal waters. Using this type of sailing required accurate charts (nautical maps) to ensure a safe voyage.

One of the many jobs of the Eighth Coast Guard District Office in New Orleans, LA was to send out a general message to all shipping called "Notice to Mariners." This message gave such information as where a new oil rig was located, buoys missing or off station, new shipwrecks, or other dangerous information. The *Gentian's* quartermaster would take this information and update our charts.

One of the interesting sights in our area of operation was getting to see one of the "mothball fleets". While working buoys in the Sabine River between Texas and Louisiana we would pass hundreds of cargo ships left over from WWII. The freighters were sealed to prevent rust and moored side by side in a wide section of the river. These ships were surplus to current needs but were being kept in case of a national emergency. Every so often one of the ships would be sold and cut up for scrap metal.

Almost all sailors get seasick if the seas are really bad. We had one seaman that would get sick every time we got underway. When we were tied up to the dock, he was a good worker, but as soon as the last mooring line was thrown of the dock, he would have to go lay down. After several hours he would get up and perform his duties, but he did not feel well the whole time we were away from the dock.

I would get seasick when the weather turned especially stormy. I would take a bucket and a wash rag with me when I had to stand OOD watch. It was not fun but there were not that many bad weather days in the Gulf. We had a lot more trouble with fog.

The city of Galveston, being on an island, had a fine beach on the ocean side. The family would often go the beach for relaxing afternoon. David had gotten over his fear of the waves by this time. On one such outing Linda and I had selected a spot where we could keep an eye on the kids while they played in the water's edge. David had on a distinctive red plaid swimsuit. As we relaxed, we look up often to see what the kids were doing. It was comforting to see that red swimsuit. When it was time to go, I went to get David, man was I surprised when the boy in the red swimsuit was not David. I had no clue where he was. After much searching, I located David half mile north on the beach. A policeman had David by the hand and was looking for his parent.

After completing one year of shipboard duty, I could now fill out a wish sheet (a form indicating where I would like to serve next). The war in Vietnam was going strong and the Coast Guard had several cutters and small patrol boats in the theater. Being young and patriotic (foolish) my first chose was to go to Vietnam. I do not remember what my next two choices were. The assignment officer in Headquarters, being much wiser than I was, cut me orders to go to the Reserve Training Center in Yorktown, VA. I was going back to where I came from.

In August 1967 Linda and I packed up our belongings, loaded up Sharon and David and headed back to tidewater Virginia. The family traveled by auto again and the furniture was shipped by commercial movers.

CHAPTER 10

DRILL INSTRUCTOR

September 1967 found Linda, Sharon, David, and I traveling back to the Norfolk, Portsmouth, Newport News, Virginia area. Linda was pregnant with our third child. Her due date was in October.

I was being assigned to the Coast Guard Reserve Training Center in Yorktown, VA. My orders stated that I would be a classroom instructor in the Officer Candidate School program. Later I found out that also meant that I would be a Drill Instructor (DI) for new officer candidates.

First order of business was to find a place to live in the Yorktown area. Linda and I began looking at the housing options. Since I had been discharged and reenlisted as an enlisted man, I was qualified to use the GI Bill. As this assignment was a three year tour, buying house seemed like a good idea. We settled on buying a house in the upper Newport News area about a twenty-five minute drive from Yorktown. The home was a small three bedroom ranch style house on a quiet dead end street. There was no garage but it did have a carport and a large back yard. The cost was about $19,000 if memory serves me correctly. It would be about two weeks before our furniture arrived, so we had to borrow temporary basic furniture from family. It was good to have Linda's folks and extended family nearby in Portsmouth, VA.

With the family settled in, it was time for me to go back to work. When I reported in I found that three more of my OCS classmates were returning as instructors. We were assigned, one each, to the four major departments. I and my classmates were Ensigns (ENS-01) when we reported for duty. On 10 December 1967 all four of us were promoted to Lieutenant Junior Grade (LTJG, O-2). Two years later 10 December 1969 I was promoted to Lieutenant (LT O-3).

None of us had experience as classroom instructors. To give us some training as classroom instructors, we were given TAD (temporary active duty) orders to a two week instructor course at Norfolk Naval Station, Norfolk, VA. I also attended a one week instructor training class at Fort Eustis an Army base in Newport News, VA. Ft Eustis was the Army's training facility for all aspects of transportation. It seems that the Army has more small boats than the Navy does. The course was designed to teach instructors how to handle themselves in a classroom, how to write lesson plans and how to teach those lessons plans. Their philosophy was "Tell them what you're going to tell them, tell them, and then tell them what you told them." In other words tell them what you expect them to learn, teach them the lesson and then summarize the main points of the lesson. After this one week class we were expected to jump from the frying pan into the fire.

At night I attended three education related college level courses at William and Mary Collage in Williamsburg, VA. Then in June of 1969 I attended a TV Instructor's Course at the Navy Schools Command at Great Lakes, Ill.

I learned that I was to be assigned to the Navigation Department. I assume I was assigned to this department because I made good navigation grades in my OCS class. There were three other instructors in the department in addition to me. The head of the department was a LCDR and the other two instructors were LTs. At first, after going to instructor school, I would monitor classes that another instructor taught. After doing this a week I taught a class for week with another instructor monitoring the class. Two weeks later I begin teaching classes by myself.

The text book for the first part of the course was Dutton's "Navigation & Piloting". Later when teaching celestial navigation the text was "Bowditch's Celestial Navigation". Each class had handouts with problems to work in the classroom as well as homework. After my first OCS class I took the handouts and organized the exercises into a workbook. The booklet had a cardstock cover and all of the problems for the entire class. I designed the cover, typed masters for the individual pages, and added a few illustrations to dress the booklet up a little. The base had its own print shop and I worked with the civilian in charge to print, collate and staple the workbooks together. This allowed the instructors to hand out a workbook at the beginning of the class instead of handouts at each class.

At first, I did not like getting up in front of the class and talking. The longer I taught, the better I became. After the first OCS class I got to where I could handle things pretty well. The biggest challenge was trying to explain a concept in a way that the students would understand. Looking at the student's faces you could see that certain people did not grasp what you were attempting to explain. That is when you had to use different examples to get the point across. Then you would have to explain the same concept two or three times to be sure that the entire class understood.

There was one particular concept that someone in each class would always ask about. It seems like the question was ask the same way in every class. After a while instead of trying to explain, we instructors would just say, "turn to page XXX in your text book, left hand side, third paragraph from the top and you will find your answer". The students appeared to be amazed that the instructor would remember exactly where they should look.

The last half of the Navigation Class was devoted to teaching celestial navigation. Celestial navigation is the science taking readings, with a sextant, of the sun, moon or stars, then calculating your position on the chart. The students would always ask why they had to learn celestial navigation since LORAN and Radio Direction Finders were commonly used in piloting and deep water sailing. We would answer, "What if the ship loses a generator and you have no electrical power. Without electricity LORAN is useless. Using sextants is your backup"

Celestial navigation was the real tough part of the course since it required a lot of math and trigonometry. This is where the text book "Bowditch's Celestial Navigation" came into play. You did not have to know how to calculate the sines and cosines. You just had to know where to look up the information in the text book and apply the information in the correct way to solve the problem you were given.

The instructors taught the theory of how to use a sextant, but the students did not do any practical training since we did not have a horizon to work with. That was left for the new officers to learn in "on the job training" once they were aboard ship. In class the students were given the sextant readings and then they had to work out the problem to find their location. The job was for the student to work the given problem to come up with a "line of site". Three of these lines, if worked correctly; would cross at a point (or at least a small triangle) on the chart and this was your position. This was not an easy task. It was common for a student to apply a correction in the wrong direction and end up plotting their position in downtown New York City.

On the final exam, the students were given three sextants sights. Their job was to work the three problems and plot their positions. This one exam was one third of the Cadets final grade for the course. Because the grade on this exam was so important, students were given partial credit if the students showed they knew how to compute the problem but made a math mistake in the calculations. The bottom line was that the four instructors had to work all the problems for approximately 120 to 140 students. The instructor would work a problem and if an error was found, the instructor would finish working the problem using the incorrect information. If everything worked out the student would be given partial credit. The more errors found the lower the score. This would take the instructors three or four, eight-hour days, to grade the exam. The day after giving the final exam we would lock the door to the office and start work. It was good that no one could hear the comments we made. There were some pretty rotten comments made about some of the students.

None of us new instructors had experience as Drill Instructors, but we were all ex enlisted. The Coast Guard's position was that we had been to boot camp, served at least six years and graduated from OCS. That gave us enough experience to teach college graduates the basics of military drill and customs. A few of the college graduates had been in ROTC programs in college. They knew the basics of marching and manual of arms. As with any new job, my first OCS class as Drill instructor (DI) had a learning curve. I just remembered how I was treated in boot Camp and in OCS and tried to do the same. I do not remember discussing how a DI should act with my class mates. Each one of us would teach as best we could. When a Cadet would make a mistake, I would get in his face and scream and holler just like I had been treated.

Just as it had been in Boot Camp and OCS, I still have some problems with dyslexia. I had to be real careful when giving marching orders. It can be embarrassing when you give a column left command when you mean column right. The troops do not like to be marched into a brick wall. This happened only once, but once was enough. I used it as a learning experience on how **not** to obey an unlawful command.

One of the DIs was short, only about 5'6". Because of his height he was a little sensitive to what other people thought of him. One day, while walking backwards calling cadence for his Company of Cadets, he stepped on uneven ground and fell. One of the Cadets snickered. He jumped up, began yelling at them because they had seen him fall. I think he made the whole company run high port around the drill field.

This same Officer had to have hemorrhoid surgery. The Doctor put him on "no duty" status and told him to stay at home for two weeks to recuperate. He was to use a donut pillow to sit on while his surgery healed. After some discussion, the Doctor said he could travel by car to his hometown in Maine. He was to do no driving, no lifting of any kind, and to be sure to use his donut pillow while riding in the car. With his wife driving He left for Maine the next day. They did not get very far when they had a flat tire. His wife had to change the tire while he gave directions. Shortly a car with four Marines stopped to help. When the Leathernecks saw a healthy looking male standing watching an obviously pregnant women trying to change a tire, they were ready to beat him up. His wife quickly explained the problem and the Marines changed the tire for them.

I did not like being yelled and screamed at when I was in Boot Camp, and I did not really like doing the same to the new Cades. However I quickly found out that the system works. The idea was to shave their heads, dress everyone in the same clothes so they all looked alike, them shout and scream to break down their spirit. Then you would work with them to build their confidence and get them to work together as a team. My first platoon I did my share of hollering in their face, and was really hard on the group. The next platoon I was a little more compassionate with the men, but after they graduated I could see the first platoon did much better than the second. After that I went back to the tried and true methods.

There was one Cadet in my third platoon that I really had problems with. He was a thin, uncoordinated, eyeglass wearing, bookish type person. He did well in class but just could not seem to be able to do the marching and manual of arms bit. He was forever making mistakes and holding the rest of the platoon up. I took him aside and worked with him one on one. He tried so hard to do the drills. I think he was trying too hard. He wanted really bad to be a Coast Guard officer. Every time he tried to do a marching maneuver, he would make a mistake. Finally in the end he realized that he could not make the grade and he resigned. I sure he made a good enlisted man in one of the technical ratings.

My officer rank was temporary as I was still officially and enlisted man. I had continued to work on my enlisted rating correspondence courses. I completed the Chief Yeoman (YNC) back in March 1963. On March 5, 1968 I was promoted to Chief Yeoman (E-7). Next year on October 13, 1969, after ten years enlisted service, I was discharged with the rank of Chief Yeoman (YNC). I now had permanent officer status as LTJG (O-2).

On October 18, 1967, my third child was born in the Norfolk Naval Hospital, in Portsmouth, VA. Her name was Darlene Francise and she was the only child that I got to be home during the delivery. After a couple of days we took Darlene home to Newport News, VA. And I went back to work. All three of my children were born in the same hospital, even though I had been to Puerto Rico, halfway across the United States and back, between the last two children.

It was about that time that we got our first dog. She was a full blood Irish Sitter named Goldie. Goldie was great with the kids and was a great mother dog of several litters. The yard had two gates, one in front under the car port and the second in back. If the front gate was left open by the kids, Goldie would stay in the yard. But if the back gate was open the dog was long gone. She would run the neighbor for half a day and then come home.

I wanted my children to a tree house to play in. I had wanted a tree house when I was small but did not get one. Alas there were no trees in our yard. To overcome this problem I took a 2 x 6 and nailed a 2 x 4 on each side. This made an I beam that was very strong. The beams were inserted upright in holes in the ground about eight feet apart. On top of this I built a small house that could be reached by a ladder. Between the columns and under the "tree house" I made a sand box. This worked out well until the older children outgrew the structure.

As it grew close to time for my tour to be over, I started to fill out my wish list for my next assignment. It was the policy of the Coast Guard that every other duty station would be aboard a cutter. I was considering asking for a 180 buoy tender in Alaska. One of my fellow instructors had served in Alaska and was telling me how beautiful the scenery was. He also said it was a great place to hunt and fish. He said that he had a lot of pictures of the Alaskan countryside. I ask him and his wife to come over for supper and bring the pictures. When he got there most of the pictures were of the great Alaskan earthquake. That clinched it for Linda. She said in no uncertain terms, that she was not going to Alaska. The next day I made some changes on my wish list.

In April 1970 I received my new orders. I was staying in the Yorktown, VA area. My new duty station was to be the USCGC *Courier* (WTR-410). The CGC *Courier* was docked at the Reserve Training Center. My family would not have to move this time.

CHAPTER 11

USCGC *COURIER* (WTR-410)

I reported on board the USCGC *Courier* (WTR-410) in April 1970 at Yorktown, VA. At the time I was a Lieutenant (LT, O-3) and had just completed a tour of duty at the Reserve Training Center. The mission of the CGC *Courier* was to provide a floating platform to train Coast Guard Reserve Port Security Units. The ship was used by the reserve units as a home base and a place to live during their two-week training period. This allowed the Reserve Unit to conduct their annual training in the port that they would be assigned to in the event they were mobilized during a national emergency. The CGC *Courier* was scheduled to sail to various ports during the summer months for two-week periods. The ship was well equipped to handle this task. In addition to providing berthing and meals for approximately 300 reservists, there was an operations office, three 30' wooden hull patrol boats and two radio-equipped cars. When moving between ports the boats were cradled on top of #2 and #3 hatch covers. The cars were stored in #1 hold between decks. Number 2 and 3 holds were converted to berthing areas.

The *Courier* was different from any other ship on which I had been assigned. She had been built as a freighter during WW-II. The bridge and superstructure were all the way aft. There were three holds forward of the bridge and one small hold aft of the superstructure. It was the engines that really fascinated me. I had been used to diesel electric propulsion systems on the buoy tenders. The CGC *Courier* had one huge diesel engine about seven or eight feet high and was direct drive through reduction gears. There were eight cylinders that were about four feet in diameter as I remember them. What really fascinated me was the fact you had to stop the engine and start it in reverse when you wanted to go astern. I could imagine the action in the engine room if the engineers got the word to go from full ahead to full astern.

The Commanding Officer of the CGC Courier was Captain (CAPT, O6) John O'Malley. I had served with CAPT O'Malley previously on the CGC *Chincoteague*. He was a Lieutenant (LT, O-3) at the time and was the First Lieutenant in charge of the deck force. I was a lowly Seaman Apprentice just out of Boot Camp. CAPT O'Malley's nickname at that time was "coach". Later on CAPT O'Malley was the senior officer on my interview board when I applied for Officer Candidate School, the second time.

The Executive Officer was CDR Ben Schaeffer. The Engineering Officer was LT Carl Kauffman. Carl and I had been in the same Office Candidate School class. Upon arriving on board I was assigned as Operations Officer and Training Officer. That meant that I was a high priced gofer. I was the liaison between the Executive Officer and the Reserve Unit training on board. I also was responsible for ordering supplies and equipment that the Reserve Unit would be using.

The first summer I was on board, the CGC Courier was scheduled for a couple of ports on the East Coast and five stops in the Great Lakes. We were to leave about May and be gone till September. One of the interesting things about the cruse to the Great Lakes was the fact that we had to modify the ship to meet environmental laws. This was just after the Cuyahoga River in Cleveland, OH had caught on fire. All the lakes and rivers in that part of the country were badly polluted. Laws had been passed that made it illegal to pump sewage into the water. LT Kauffman had been working night and day to design plans and install a holding tank and pumps to accommodate 300 plus people. After all this had been done there was a kink in the plans as usual. After the Coast Guard had modified the CGC Courier to comply with the law, we found out that the dockside facilities had not. LT Kauffman had to go back to the drawing board and figure a way to get rid of our waste. The solution was to use hundreds of feet of hose to pump affluent to a distant opening to the local sewer system. As soon as we moored, out would swarm the engineering department, dragging their black, hard rubber hoses, looking for the closest manhole cover for the sewer system.

The first port–of-call that summer was in New Bedford CT. We were there for the regular two-week period then went back to Norfolk, VA. It was a short stay in a shipyard to work on the holding tanks. That gave us a chance to spend a little extra time with our families.

On departing from Norfolk in June 1970 we were involved in a collision with another ship. The Courier had just passed over the tunnel to the Chesapeake Bay Bridge/Tunnel complex. I had just been relieved as Officer of the Deck. We were meeting this Navy ship, the USS *Pocono* (AGC-16). headed for The Navy Amphibious Base at Little Creek, VA. After watching the USS *Pocono,* the OOD saw that we were on a converging course. The OOD sounded a signal of one short blast which indicated that he planned to pass port to port. The *Pocono* answered with one blast that indicated that they agreed we would pass port to port. For some reason the *Pocono* did not change course as expected. The Captain immediately relieved the OOD on the bridge. As required by the nautical Rules of the Road the Captain continued on our same course, until we were "in extremis". The Captain then signaled the engine room for full astern, but there was not enough time to avoid the collusion with the other ship. It takes the *Courier* a full mile to come to a complete stop. The collision alarm sounded, and it was announced over the PA system for everyone to grab a handhold. I had just left the bridge and was one deck down. I set down on the deck and held on tight. The USS *Pocono* hit us, bow to bow on the port anchor. The 5/8" steel of our deck plates was curled up like a pretzel. The bulk of the anchor was on the bottom without the chain. Only one person was hurt on the CGC *Courier.* He had been sitting on a chair and fell off, injuring his arm. Needless to say we turned around and went back to Norfolk to have our bow repaired and to wait for a Board of Investigation. The interesting part of the proceedings was that the Coast Guard held a Board for the *Courier,* and the Navy held a Board for the *Pocono.* Then the two services got together and compared notes. At least that was what we were told. CAPT O'Malley was not held responsible for the collision. The repairs did cause the ship to miss one training session.

CGC *Courier* collusion

Finally, all the repairs were done, and we headed for the Great Lakes. I do not remember much about the trip up and around Nova Scotia and New Brunswick. It must have been like any other sea voyage, standing watch, trying to get work done and sleep. Travelling up the St. Lawrence Seaway was something I had not done before. Once we got past Quebec, we took on a French speaking pilot. He could not speak much English and we did not have anyone who could speak French. However, he was used to the language problem and took control of things.

The first thing he did was tell the helmsman to go get a cup of coffee and stay out of his way. The pilot took over the helm himself. When he needed to see what was going on he left the helm unattended (a practice I had not heard of before), walked out on the wing of the bridge, had his look around, then went back and started steering again. This action made the OOD very nervous. Looking back, with the benefit of years, I realize his action was a simple way to eliminate the chance of a misunderstood order because of the language problem.

It was a beautiful trip up the St. Lawrence Seaway, especially the Thousand Island area between New York and Canada. There were hundreds and hundreds of small green islands jam packed with summer houses. There were small boats all over the place. I had not heard of this area before, but it was one of the regions summer resort areas. The scenery was beautiful, and I bet the fishing was good.

We had one of the boats play chicken with us. This small outboard came up and ran alongside the ship. Then he would cut across the bow to get to the other side. He was so close that we would lose sight of him from the bridge. The bridge was at the back of the 310' ship and with the high bow there was a large blind spot in front. Every now and then we noticed that his outboard would stop, and he had to crank the engine several times to get it started again. Then his engine stopped while he was in the bind spot. The Chief Boatswain in charge of the anchor detail said he was really cranking on the starter rope while keeping an eye of the ship bearing down on him. There was no way for us to stop. Finally, he got the engine started and got out of the way. After that he didn't stick around and play chicken anymore. The Pilot took the registration number off the boat and said he would report the incident to the Canadian authorities.

Our first port was Cleveland, OH. We spent one two-week training period there. There isn't anything that sticks out in my memory about Cleveland. The Reserve Unit came on board on Sunday afternoon. We off-loaded the 30' patrol boats, the radio-equipped cars, and broke out the sewer hoses. Monday morning the Reserves started their patrols and other training activities. The officers from the Reserve Unit organized and conducted all the training activities. The reserve personnel slept on board. The ship feed the men and provided logistic support. The crew of the *Courier*, except the duty section, was given liberty each evening. Saturday morning, two weeks later, the Reservist left. We loaded up our gear, unhooked the sewer hoses and on Saturday evening left port and steamed overnight to our next port of call.

The next stop was Detroit, where we stayed four weeks and trained two different Port Security Units. The Courier moored right downtown. I think the dock where we tied up is now the Convention and Preforming Arts Center. The one thing I remember about downtown Detroit was how dark and dingy the buildings looked. This was because of all the smoke and smog that had settled on the buildings I was told. I have since heard that many of the buildings were cleaned up.

Two things I enjoyed about Detroit were going across the river to Windsor, Canada to have dinner and the second was visiting the Henry Ford Museum. Visiting Windsor was my first and only time to step on Canadian soil. I take that back. Earlier tin my career I visited Argentia, Newfoundland when I was on a weather patrol cutter in the North Atlantic. Since we never left the U.S. Naval Base, it did not seem like we were in Canada.

The next port of call was Milwaukee, WI. This meant steaming through Lake Huron, the Straits of Mackinac and into Lake Michigan. Lake Superior was the only one of the Great Lakes that we did not visit. The stop in Milwaukee was for two weeks and was just a repeat on the first three training sessions, just a different group of reservists.

At Chicago we tied up at what was called the Navy pier. For the crew of the *Courier*, one training period was just like ones before, just another day at the office.

The one thing that was different in Chicago was that a local doctor invited all the ship's officers over for a cocktail party (Sorry

I don't remember the doctor's name). He had been stationed on the CGC *Courier* while she was the Voice of America in Rhodes, Greece. The doctor hired a limousine to come pick us up. The driver really laid on the red-carpet treatment, literally. He drove up to the gangway, played his musical horn, then jumped out and got a roll of red carpet from the trunk. He rolled the carpet from the car up to the gangway. When the musical horn played everyone ran over to that side of the ship to see what was going on. I'll swear that the ship took a 10-degree list to the dock side. The Party was really terrific, and everyone had a good time.

While at Milwaukee we had a change of command. CAPT O'Malley left for another assignment and CDR Schaeffer moved up to Commanding Officer. LCRD McBride reported on board as Executive Officer. CDR Schaeffer's wife, LT Kauffman's wife and my wife drove up from Newport News, VA for a weeklong visit and for the change of command. The Wisconsin State Fair was going on at the time and all six of us enjoyed an afternoon at the fair.

CDR Schaeffer and LT Kauffman were both from a German background. Milwaukee has a large German population. CDR Schaeffer and LT Kauffman decided they both wanted to eat some authentic German food. I recall we were at a local barbershop, getting haircuts, at the time of this discussion. We ask the barber where we could get the best German food in town. The barber said take the street out front, travel south until we thought we were lost, and we would be at the best restaurant in town. (I do not remember the name of the restaurant). That night all six of us piled into the car and headed south. Shortly the houses started getting farther and farther apart. Soon there were no houses and just a few cows here and there. We had decided that we must have missed the restaurant. About that time we came over the top of a hill. On the far side of the valley was a group of lights. It was decided to drive to the lights to turn around and go back to town. When we arrived at the lights, there was the restaurant we were looking for. We had a great time that night. The food was good, dancing was wonderful, and Grandma was over from the old country to entertain us on the harpsichord. After the Change of command, the wives left for home, and we went back to work.

When we finished the two weeks stay in Chicago, it was back to Yorktown, VA for the winter. There was a lot of maintenance and other work to get ready for the next summer. One of the jobs was overhauling the automobiles and the 30' patrol boats. There had been breakdowns a few times during the summer and cars and boats were kept going with temporary repairs. Of course, there is always chipping the rust and panting that has to be done. Old crewman left and new ones came aboard. Not much leave was allowed during the summer, so everyone took time off during the winter.

During the last part of 1970 the Executive Officer, LCDR McBride, was in a serious automobile accident. His leg was very badly broken. Even after a long spell in the hospital and on sick leave, he had to walk with a cane for a long time. You can imagine what it was like trying to get up and down ship's ladders with a cane. While he was on sick leave I was designated as acting Executive Officer. I was kept busy trying to do the Executive Officer's job and mine also.

I expected to get transferred at the end of the summer cruse in 197l. After much discussion with Linda, we decided to move her and the children out to Oklahoma for the long summer. My family had not seen much of Linda and the children, so this gave them a chance to get better acquainted. We put the furniture in storage and the family, and I drove out to Oklahoma. I had a Volkswagen bug at the time. It was fun with two adults, three kids and an Irish setter dog. Travel was going well until we passed a flock of birds. One of the kids yelled "Goldie quit pointing, there is not enough room". The family had a good time that summer meeting all the aunts, uncles, and cousins. I dumped them off and went back to Yorktown to get ready for more sea time.

The second summer I knew more about what to expect, so it was not as difficult to make preparations. When we got underway that spring our first stop was in Galveston, TX. After two weeks there, we spent four weeks in New Orleans. LA. After that came Tampa, FL, Miami, FL and Charleston, SC. Seems like there were one or two more stops but I don't remember them. They all started to blend together.

One of my memories is of the amount of time the deck force spent repairing the hulls of the patrol boats. The reserve boat crews ran aground numerous times, especially in Charleston harbor where there was a lot of shallow water. The crew spent many hours sanding the hulls and applying a new fiberglass coating.

Another memory is of the seaman that refused to take required test for advancement to Boatswain Mate third class. His stated reason was that he did not want the responsibility, even though it meant more money for him. The odd thing was that he was very knowledgeable and often put in charge of working parties. He often carried out the duties of a third-class petty office, but still he didn't want the responsibility.

On the Courier we had a saying in the wardroom, "every day is a Monday, but every night is a Saturday night." We did like to go out, have a good time and let off steam. I can remember going to morning muster at 8:00 a.m., working all day, and then having dinner at 5:00 p.m. After dinner I would lie down and sleep till bout 7:30 or 8. After a quick shower, I would go ashore, usually with a group, and hang out in one of the local bars until 2 or 3 in the morning. After few hours' sleep the routine would start all over again. The only break in the routine was steaming from one port to another.

I transferred to a new assignment in September 1971. My new job was to be the Executive Officer on a 180' buoy tender in Mobile, AL.

CHAPTER 12

USCGC BLACKTHORN (WLB 391)

I departed the CGC *Courier* on September 18, 1971. For travel in route I was authorize 2 days travel time and 30 days leave. My wife and children were living in Oklahoma so I flew there first. After saying good bye to my Mother and two siblings, my family and I drove to Mobile, AL. We still had the Volkswagen bug and travel was crowded. Upon arrival in Mobile, Linda and I went house hunting. We rented a nice four bedroom home from a military couple that was on assignment overseas. The houses had a very nice shaded yard. The house had a red double door and a hallway that was wide enough you could store a dining room table while cleaning floors. Our furniture was in storage in Newport News, VA, so I arranged for it to be shipped to Mobile.

With my leave over I reported on board the USCGC *Blackthorn* (WLB-391) on October 18, 1971. I was a Lieutenant when I arrived and my assignment was to relieve the Executive Officer. My job placed me second in command of the ship. I was expected to carry out the Captain's, orders-even if I disagreed with them,-oversee operations of the ship, maintain good discipline and order, and to act as Personnel Officer.

USCGC *Blackthorn* (WLB-391)

The *Blackthorn* was a 180' deep sea buoy tender. Our area of operation was the entrance to Mobile Bay and east to Apalachicola in the Florida panhandle, including the major channels in between. One of the major channels was at Pensacola, FL where the Navy trained a lot of their pilots.

The ship tied up at the Coast Guard Base on the south side of Mobile harbor. Mobile is located on the northern edge of Mobile Bay. It was a 30 mile trip from the dock to the sea buoy at the entrance to the ship channel. The bay was very shallow and large ships had to stay in the channel.

A sister ship, the USCGC *Salvia* (WLB-400), also moored in Mobile. Her area of operation was west from Mobile Bay to the mouth of the Mississippi.

After meeting the Captain and having an interview with him, it was time to start the process of relieving the Executive Officer.

First we set down in the ship's office and went over the paperwork and files. I met the yeoman that would be my assistant. Next came a tour of the ship and the XO explained the projects that were underway. Since I had served on two other 1l80' buoy tenders--Once as enlisted and then as an Ensign, I had a good idea the normal routine. It was items unique to the *Blackthorn* where I needed to be brought up to speed. During the tour I was introduced to senior petty officers and many of the crew. At lunch time I got acquainted with the other officers in the wardroom.

I had reported for duty on a Monday and the next day the *Blackthorn* got underway to work buoys in one of the harbors. As we proceeded up the channel I was the OOD and the XO was by my side to give advice about local conditions. The Captain was also on the bridge. We were to work in a branch channel that made a sharp turn to the left. Looking at the chart and the display on the radar, I said it was time to start our turn to the port. The XO said "no we should wait a little bit" which I did. Technically as OOD, I was in charge and should have followed my instincts.

When we finally made the turn to the port, the ship came to slow stop, aground in soft mud. I was a little slow in reacting and the Captain relieved me of the CON. He immediately gave the order for full astern and ordered the helm to be shifted full starboard to full port and back again several times. The idea was to rock the boat from right to left to loosen the suction of the mud. The ship paused for a few minutes and then began to move, slowly at first, then faster as we backed off the mud bank. Once we were back into the channel, the Captain sent the Chief Boatswain Mate to check the lower hole and the chain locker in the bow. There were no signs of a leak. Next order of business was to send a message to the Eighth District Office notifying them that the ship had been aground.

Instead of finishing our work that week, we returned to port. The next day we had a diver check the bottom of ship for damage. It turned out that there were some miner dents in the hull but no major damage. More important there were no leaks. It was lucky that the bottom of the channel was mud and not rocks.

So much for working buoys that week. I finished relieving the XO and he departed for his next duty station and some leave. I was now officially the Executive Officer of the *Blackthorn* for the next year and half.

Working buoys was the same as the other ships I was on. We would pull up beside a buoy, hook on, and lift it onto the deck. The deck crew would scrape the bottom, paint if necessary, replace the batteries and check the light bulbs. There were four light bulbs on the buoy. They were installed in a mechanism that when a bulb burned out, it would automatically rotate another good bulb in place and keep on shining bright. There was a daylight sensor that would turn the bulb off during the day, thus saving battery power. When the buoy was checked out, the crew would check the chain and sinker. The OOD would maneuver the ship into position and the buoy would be dropped on location. Then on to the next buoy and repeat the operation. There were times when the ship would be work some buoys and we would send a boat crew to check minor problems on other buoys nearby.

Things did not always go as the Captain planned. We would be right in the middle of work in one area and we would get a message that a buoy was off station in another location. We would have to stop work, or wait till the end of the day, then steam over to take care of the problem. Fog was another problem on the Gulf Coast. Some mornings the fog was so thick that we could not see to take bearings needed to locate the buoy properly. We would have to wait for the fog to clear or steam to another work location. Someone would ask "what are we going to do today" and someone else would answer "play it by ear". Soon "play it by ear" became our unofficial slogan. One day a picture of an ear, with the slogan underneath, showed up on the bulletin board in the mess hall.

There was one week where things got really bad. The *Blackthorn* got underway on Monday with the intention of working near Panama City, FL. When we got to Panama City the fog was so dense that we could not work. While waiting for the fog to lift we received a message that several buoys, in the bypass ship channel from New Orleans, were off station. This was the work area for the CGC *Salvia* but she could not get underway because of mechanical problems. We steamed over to the Mississippi delta. When we got there the fog was too bad to work. The weather report indicated that there would be heavy fog for a couple for days. It also reported that the fog had cleared at Panama City, so we headed back to that area. When we arrived back at Panama City, you guessed it, the fog was back. But the fog had cleared in the area of the Mississippi River Delta. Not when we got there. The whole week was like that. Finally on Friday the Captain said enough of this, we're going back home.

When we arrived at the Mobile sea buoy, late in the evening, the fog was very thick. The Captain decided to anchor for the night. Just as we were ready to secure from the anchor detail, the lookout announced that an oil tanker was inbound for the sea buoy. The Captain kept an eye on the tanker to see what his intentions were. Slowly the ship kept coming until it was clear that she intended to proceed up the channel. The anchor was ordered brought back aboard; since the Captain had decided that we would follow the tanker up the channel.

No sooner had we sailed passed the barrier island than we came upon the tanker, aground on the right side of the channel. After determining that the Skipper of the tanker did not need assistance, the *Blackthorn* slowly eased around the tanker and continued up the channel. By this time we were committed. We couldn't anchor in the channel and it was too fogy to turn around and go back outside.

That was a very slow trip up the ship channel. The *Blackthorn* was making only about three knots. We had lookouts on both wings of the bridge trying to spot the channel markers. The fog was so thick we only had about 100 yard visibility. The Captain was conning the ship and I was on the radar. I was watching for outbound traffic and looking for the next channel marker. The lookouts would identify the number on the marker and the quartermaster would check it off on the chart. That way we would know exactly where we were in the channel. Without a mishap we made it to the channel that turned left into our mooring basin. We carefully made our turn. The ship was almost to the dock before we could see the lights on the warehouse on the dock. We had sent a message to the local Coast Guard base about the conditions and they had notified some of the wives. Several of the wives met us on the dock. That was a knight that I didn't forget.

They say that grass is greener on the other side of the fence. I noticed an event that proved that point. The CGC *Salvia* was the same class buoy tinder as the *Blackthorn* and had the same size crew. If one of our crew members had a meal on the *Salvia*, he would brag about how good the food was. When a member of the *Salvia* came over to eat with us, he would brag on our chow. When you get use to the food being prepared and seasoned the same way day after day, and then you get to eat at a different location the food just taste better.

About half way through our stay in Mobile my family had to move. The couple that owned the house we were renting, came back early. After scouting the area we found a small two bedroom house. This house also had a shaded yard, but this time there was also a vacant yard next door. While this house was much smaller than the first one, this house felt more like home.

My youngest daughter, Darlene, was about four years old at that time. She loved all animals and would play with roly-polies, ants and other insects. One day I was out working in the yard when Darlene came around the corner of the house hollering "worms, daddy worms". I followed her back around the corner and found her point to a snake about three feet long. I quickly took her inside and got rid of the snake.

I had a chance to take my son, David, out fishing on one of the piers in Mobile Bay. On one occasion I remember him catching a fish. It was a good size sea bass. I'm sure we caught other fish but that is the only one that I remember.

Then there was the time that Darlene saw a monkey in a pet store. I did not buy the monkey right then and she thru a fit. I told her to forget the monkey and took her home. Later I went back and purchased the animal. I thought it would be a good pet for the kids to play with. Wrong!!

When I brought the monkey home in a cardboard box, Linda asked me what I planned to do with it. I had not thought that far ahead. While we were discussing the situation, the monkey escaped form the box and went tearing around the house. We caught the critter after it had fallen in a big pot of oil in the kitchen. I took the well-oiled brat and put him in the bathroom and shut the door. Then I left to purchase material to build a cage.

When I got the cage built I went to get the monkey. I found

that he had wrecked the bathroom. Among other things he had torn down the shower curtain and eaten a bar of soap. He sat on the edge of the tub blowing soap bubbles. With a little bit of fight, we finally got him into the cage. Meanwhile the kids were laughing and having a good old time.

Originally we put the cage in the bedroom where Sharon and Darlene slept. That did not work out. Darlene was not much bigger than the monkey and he tried to dominate her. Every time she would come into the room he would start screaming and having a fit. He was strong enough that he could bite a whole in a stainless steel food bowl. I was afraid he might grab her and bite her. The cage had to go to another location.

David's bed was in a small room between the living room and kitchen. We decided to relocate the monkey there. One evening we were watching the TV. One of us looked around and said look at the monkey. He had found a way to open the cage door. He was leaning out of the cage, looking around the door jamb, watching TV with us. I quickly got him back into the cage and found a better way to lock the door.

It was while we were living in the small home that Goldie, our purebred Irish setter dog, was pregnant again. We had bred her to another purebred dog and hoped to get a nice litter of pups. Goldie had raised two other litters and both times the litters were large, ten or twelve. This time Goldie gave birth to fifteen pups. After three days two of the pups died. We took mom and the remainder of the litter to a veterinarian to see what the problem was. He diagnosed her with milk fever. The vet's prescription was to take the puppies away from mother for three days and hand feed them. Mother was to be fed fried liver twice a day for the three days. You have to understand, Linda had made a pact when we got married, no fried liver in the house. Goldie tried to tear the door down trying to get to her puppies. Somehow we made it through the three day ordeal. It was not easy. Goldie made the newspaper for having such a large litter. There was even a photo of Darlene playing with the brood of pups.

One of the duties of the Executive Officer was being the Personnel Officer for the ship. This included having to council young coasties just out of boot camp. It seems the first thing they wanted to do when the reported aboard, was to ask for a transfer closer to home. There was usually a girl involved. I tried to tell them that they could always go home at the end of their four year enlistment. Now was time to let the U.S. government pay for them to see a new part of this great country of ours. That advice usually did go over very well. I would try to help them make the best of their time aboard ship.

I did not always agree with some of the policy decisions that the Captain made. If I didn't agree we would discuss these differences, in private, in his cabin. I remembered the one ship where the captain and the executive officer would complain to the crew about each other. That had a bad effect on the moral of the crew. After I left the Captain's cabin, I would back the Captain's decision 100%. This was not always easy, but it was the best way to go.

The CGC *Blackthorn* was ordered to proceed to the CG Yard in Curtis Bay Maryland to undergo some major repairs. Curtis Bay was near Baltimore, MD. The voyage to Curtis Bay was uneventful. I remember the passage between Key West, FL and Cuba. It was a quiet night with a very bright moon. What I remember most was seeing other ships sailing the opposite direction. They would be all lit-up and would glide silently across the water. I really enjoyed being on watch at night when the seas were calm.

The stay in the CG Yard was uneventful. We had some major repairs done in the engine room. The shipyard workers at Curtis Bay were polite and hard working. In no time the repairs were completed and it was time to return home. In the meantime the crew got to have liberty in a different location.

Our return voyage home was a little more exciting. We had a 45 foot AToN boat on board as deck cargo. As we reached the area off North Carolina we encountered a strong storm and heavy seas. The *Blackthorn* normally steamed at 10 knots and we had 30 to 40 knot headwinds. The result was that we had green water breaking over our bow. The AToN boat had an open well deck that was starting to fill up with water. If the boat got too much water on board it would affect our center of gravity and potentially cause the *Blackthorn* to capsize. We slowed to 5 knots which lessened the spray coming over the bow. With our 5 knot speed, to keep the bow into the wind, and a wind of 30 knots blowing toward us, we were actually going backward over the ground. This made for a very rough night. I had to carry my bucket with me while I was on watch. The next day the winds calmed down and the rest of the trip was uneventful.

While moving to Mobile I had been driving a VW Bug. One evening, about three months after arriving in Mobile, while heading for home my car gave up on me. I blew the engine while driving down the highway. I got the car towed to a safe spot and the next day I went looking for a new car. I was tired of trying to fit my family of five and a dog in a small car, so I started looking for something a little bigger. I found what I needed, a ford station wagon.

The next problem was figuring out the financing to pay for it. I had enough savings for the down payment, taxes and license, but I need a loan for the balance. I went to a bank where I had recently opened a checking account. It just so happened that I was in uniform. When I ask about a loan, I was taken to a loan officer. When He saw my uniform, he ask what I needed. He bent over backward to get the paperwork done and a check in my hand. The loan officer was very familiar with the Coast Guard and I could do no wrong. That was the easiest loan I ever made.

One evening the Captain gave a party at his home for the officers and crew. We had a good time that night. There was plenty of food and drinks to go around. At about 10 p.m. the Captain left for a few minutes. When he came back he was in his pajamas. He said the food is on the table, the drinks are on the counter, you all stay as long as you like. Me, I'm going to bed, by. We got the message, said our good nights and started to leave.

In April 1973 my relief reported aboard. After a tour of the ship, review of the paperwork and a review of all outstanding projects, I was relieved as Executive Officer. I packed up the furniture, loaded my family in the station wagon and we headed for my next duty station in Salt Lake City, UT.

CHAPTER 13

SALT LAKE CITY

I received orders to be the Assistant Director of Auxiliary for the state of Utah. My wife and I elected to take some of my leave and travel time and drive to Utah. We stopped off in Oklahoma to visit my mother and family. After visiting for several days, it was off on a new adventure. We traveled across southern Kansas and Colorado on US 50 highway. This route took us through Wichita and Dodge City, KS; Pueblo, Royal Gorge and Grand Junction, CO; and Provo, UT. Upon arriving in Salt Lake City our first order of business was to find a place to live.

My Wife and I found a place to live in Sandy, UT. The house was a nice split-level home on a dead-end street. There was a large open field behind the house. Our new home was about a 30-minute commute to my office in downtown Salt Lake City. If I wanted to leave the car for my wife to use, there was bus transportation available.

Sandy was a nice suburb south of downtown Salt Lake City. The Wasatch Mountain range formed the eastern city limits for both Salt Lake City and Sandy. The elevation is about 5,000 feet altitude with the mountains rising to about 8 to 9 thousand feet. The main street for Sandy was the road that went up Little Cottonwood Canyon, one of the main ski areas in Utah. There were also seven other canyons in the mountains boarding Salt Lake City, one of which is where Interstate Highway 80 comes into town.

Salt Lake City is beautiful, and the streets are laid out in a north, south, and east, west grid pattern. This makes it very easy to find an address. Main Street downtown was very wide. The rumor was that it was laid out this wide so a team of mules and wagon could turn around on it. Right downtown, in addition to the state capital building, was the Mormon Temple. There was also a tall high rise office building for the Mormon Church Headquarters.

Having found a place to live, I flew to San Francisco to report for duty. I reported to the Personnel Office at the Headquarters, 12th Coast Guard District. There they processed my permanent change of station orders, travel vouchers and other necessary paperwork.

My boss would be the Director of Auxiliary for the 12^{h} Coast Guard District. After an interview with my new boss, I flew back to Salt Lake City. I would be the only active-duty Coast Guard officer in Utah. There were two enlisted Coast Guardsmen (a chief petty officer and a 2nd class petty officer) that maned the Coast Guard recruiting office. While the Recruiters and I would share an office space in the Federal Building, in downtown Salt Lake City, they were an independent unit and did not report to me.

The CG Auxiliary is a civilian arm of the Coast Guard. established by Congress in 1939. The Auxiliary has units in all 50 states, Puerto Rico, the Virgin Islands, American Samos, and Guam. The mission is to promote and improve recreational boating safety. They do this by teach boating safety classes to recreational boaters and give voluntary boat inspections for the required safety equipment. The Auxiliary also provides trained crews and facilities to augment the Coast Guard and enhance safety and security of our ports, waterways, and coastal regions. There are several large freshwater lakes in the Utah and Wyoming area. If memory serves me correctly there were five Auxiliary flotillas in the Utah area.

My duties as Assistant Director of Auxiliary was to provide support and assistance to the five flotillas in the area. This included periodic visits to flotillas meetings, help procure educational materials and supplies, assist in coordinating programs to conduct safety equipment examinations of recreational boats at local marinas or on the water. The job also required coordinating with law enforcement personnel and other local officials. I was assisted in this work with the Auxiliary Vice Commodore West and Auxiliary District Captain.

While there were some sail boats on the Great Salt Lake, most of the power boats did their cruising on four large freshwater lakes in the area. North and West of the city there was Bear Lake and Flaming Gorge on the Wyoming boarder. South of Salt Lake City, near Provo, was Utah Lake. Then on the southern border of Utah was Lake Powell. There were also other small reservoirs around the state.

Once a month I would fly to San Francisco for an 12th District Auxiliary planning meeting. Usually, the two Auxiliary officers, the Vice Commodore West and District Captain, would accompany me on the overnight trip. We would fly to San Francisco in the afternoon, have a business meeting in the evening and fly back to Utah the next day.

We always stayed in the same hotel. The hotel had a small grill for meals. Upon arrival we would get a quick meal at the grill counter. The cook, behind the counter, was poetry in motion. His movements were very smooth as he moved from one task to another. After our evening meeting we would stop at the grill for a late-night snack. The same cook was behind counter. The next morning, we stopped for breakfast before heading to the airport. Guess what? The same cook was behind the counter. After seeing this for a couple of months I ask him, "Do you live here?" He laughed and said, me and my twin brother both cook here. Mystery solved.

One year, when the National Auxiliary Conference was held in San Francisco, the District Commander decided to bring some of the Utah auxiliarist down to the conference. He sent a Coast Guard C-130 airplane to fly us down and back. When we got on the plane at the airport there was a mechanical problem that delayed departure or a couple of hours. Once the problem was fixed everything went smooth, although setting on web seats in a military aircraft is not necessarily smooth. I always said that the trip you talk about most, is the one where something went wrong.

The most difficult job I had in Utah was to notify parents that one of their children had died. It was late one evening when I got a call from the 8th Coast Guard District that a young Coastguard's man had drowned in an accident while working AtoN (Aids to Navigation). The District Duty Officer could not give many details, just that the young man had fallen overboard. He had attempted to swim to a nearby buoy but drowned before he reached the buoy. I was to go notify the parents immediately before they heard the news from another source. The officer gave the names and address of the mother and father. Nothing in my Coast Guard training had prepared me for this kind of situation.

I hurriedly put on my dress uniform and told my wife I would be back later. Since it was clear that the parents were divorced, I elected to tell the father first. With the grid system that the city was laid out in, I was able to find the fathers home right away. I knocked on his door, introduced myself and gave him the sad news. Of course, the father was distraught over his son's death. He kept asking me questions that I could not answer because I did not know the details of the accident. When he calmed down a little, I gave him my office telephone number and suggested he call me the next day. Now it was time for me to leave him to go notify the boy's mother. The father suggested that he go with me to his ex-wife's house. Apparently, they had a civil relationship after the divorce.

Notifying the mother was even worse than telling the father. I was sure glad he was with me. Naturally the mother was very upset to learn of her son's death. She kept crying and screaming that it couldn't have happened. The mother could not understand why the boy had drown. It seems that the boy had been on the swim team in high school and was a very good swimmer. I suspected that hypothermia had something to do with the accident, but I did not have details to share with the family. After a while there nothing more I could do to help. The father decided to stay and help comfort his ex-wife and I departed.

Not long after that I had my own problem to deal with. I had ridden the city bus to work one weekday. Around 1 p.m. I started to feel nervous and found it difficult to sit still. I paced back and forth in my office to try to calm my nerves. When I set down, I would feel bad again. After about 45 minutes I decided to catch a bus and go home to rest. When I got to the bus stop, I had to wait several minutes before the bus arrived. Again, I was so nervous I could only pace up and down. Finally, the bus arrived, and I started home.

About halfway home I could feel my stomach churning and knew I was about to throw up. Sea sickness trains you about an upset stomach. I pulled the emergency cord to stop the bus. We were at a small park, I got off and went behind a tree and heaved. All I could think of was that since I was in uniform, people would think, there goes another drunk sailor.

The content of my stomach was like coffee grounds. I had never seen anything like that before. By now I was feeling a little better. I called my wife and ask her to come and pick me up. When she arrived, I told her what had happened and ask her to take me to Emergency Room at the University of Utah Hospital. At the emergency room I explained my problem, and they checked me in. The nurse led me to an examining room and told me to put on a hospital gown. She told me to lie down, that someone would be with me soon and left the room. My wife and I waited for at least 45 minutes, seemed like longer but no one came back. By then I was feeling better, and I got mad since no one had come back to check on me. After getting dressed, I stopped by the nurse's station to tell them I was leaving. The nurse got excited and ask me to wait. She wanted to know what the problem was. I told her that I had been in the treatment room for a long time, and no one even stocked their head in the door. I could have died in there. The nurse apologized and said that there had been a multi-car accident with serious injuries. She ask me to stay and someone would take care of me as soon as possible. I went back to the room. It was another hour before an emergency doctor could see me. Someone did stick their head in the door every 10 to 15 minutes to see if I was still ok.

The doctor visited with me about the systems I was having, and he had an orderly pump my stomach. Then the doctor stated that as he suspected I was having an ulcer attack and there was internal bleeding. He prescribed 4 days in the hospital so they could keep an eye on the bleeding to be sure that it did not become serious. Since I was active military, I was transferred to a military hospital. They arranged for an ambulance, and I took a 45-mile ride to Hill Air Force Base near Ogdon, UT, just north of Salt Lake City.

During my stay in Utah, I meet many interesting people. The climate and countryside were completely different from what I was used to on the Atlantic and Gulf coast. The climate was very dry, and you had to watch out for oxygen starvation in the high altitude. I particularly enjoyed exploring the front range canyons on the eastern edge of the city. I lived at about 5000 feet elevation but in just a thirty-minute drive I could be up to 8000 or 9000 feet. I remember one July about picnicking up on the high meadows and putting a six pack of soda in a snowbank on the north side of a mountain peak.

If you traveled west from Salt Lake City, you came to the salt flats and the Great Salt Lake. They say the lake was so salty that you did not swim, you would just float. I did not try to find out. Just south of the salt flat was a small mountain range. Here was one of the country's largest open-pit copper mine. The ore trucks were so big that the tires were taller than I was, yet when you see them at the bottom of the mine, they looked like ants.

To the east, In the other direction, you had high aird plains. One of the Auxiliary Flotilla Commanders operated a marina on Flaming Gorge, a large reservoir on the Green River. Upon leaving Green River, WY, on Interstate 80, you drove south twenty to thirty miles to the marina. You did not see a tree once you left the town of Green River. All could see was low growing shrubs and tumble weeds. If you took time to walk away from the road all you could see small colorful flowers hidden by the taller bushes. Once you were on the water and traveled down the lake you would be between gorge walls at least 8 or 9 hundred feet high.

A lot of the area in the West was government land managed by the BLM (Bureau of Land Management.) During my second year in Utah, I had the opportunity take a float trip down the Green River with some BLM rangers. It was an orientation trip for some new employees. We were to be gone for four days. We put in the river below the Flaming Gorge Dam near Vernal, UT. From there we would float, by raft. to a takeout point just before Green River, UT where the river joins the Colorado River.

The first night we camped at an abandon farm. Originally the settlers rafted equipment and supplies down river to the homestead. Later, supplies hauled in by mules over the mountains. There was no record of when the homestead was abandoned, but some of the horse drawn farm equipment had rubber tires.

The next day we encountered two small rapids then one medium and one good size rapids. After the second large rapid we found a damaged canoe on the bank of the river. Since it was getting late, we decided to camp for the night. The BLM rangers wanted to find out if someone from the canoe was injured since we were a long way from civilization. As it got dark, we could see a light in the far distance. Two of the BLM officers hiked over to the light to see if they could find any information. When they came back, they said the occupants of the canoe were safe. It seems the people had rented the canoe. They were told to look out for three rapids. No one told them to look out for the larger size rapids and ignore the smaller ones. The tourist went over two small rapids and the medium rapid ok. They were not prepared for the next large rapid and that is when they got into trouble. After capsizing and losing all their gear and wrecking the canoe, they called it quits and hiked out.

The next night was our last and we camped not far from the takeout point. At this location we found a large bull-snake. Bull-snakes are nonvenomous but are one of the larger snakes in North America. I was able to catch the snake and decided to take it home for my children since they liked pets of all kinds. I carried the snake in a large plastic bag. This was ok until about halfway home on the long drive. It is hard to hold the top of a bag when you fall asleep. Things got a little excited when the snake started to crawl out of the bag.

Another exciting adventure was going up anti-gravity hill. Just north of the Capital building was a road that went up the foothills to the top of a ravine. At the top it took a 180-degree hairpin turn and went down the other side. If you Looked around, it appeared that you were going downhill to the turn, but if you took your foot off the brake the car would start to slowly roll backward uphill. It was fun to take visitors there and watch their expression when the car starts rolling uphill.

During my last six months in Utah things became a little awkward. Two of the senior Auxiliarist began feuding with each other. I tried to remain neutral in the argument but that did not work out. If I did not agree with one or the other, they would think I was taking the other side. The feud was still going on when I left.

While working with the Auxiliarist, I found that the training and education materials had been developed by different people at different times. There was no systematic approach to the training process. After studying the published materials and talking to the

Auxiliarist about their training needs. I came up with some Ideas on how to improve the training text. I wrote a position paper on how I thought the training materials could be improved and organized to get better results. I sent the position paper, via the chain of command, to the Coast Guard Headquarters, Auxiliary office in Washington D.C.

Apparently, someone liked what I had written because when it came time for me to be transferred, I received orders to report to the Chief, Auxiliary and Education Division, Office of Boating Safety, Coast Guard Headquarters. My wife and I loaded up the kids, packed the car and headed for Washington, D.C.

CHAPTER 14

WASHINGTON, D.C.

My oldest daughter, Sharon, looked out the widow and suddenly said, trees, look daddy trees. She had just become awake up from a long nap. I was driving down Interstate 80 in Eastern Ohio, and the scenery was a big change from Utah. In Utah the trees were tall slim pine or alpine. Here the trees were broad leaf hardwood trees, very different from what we had been seeing the last three years.

Upon reporting at Coast Guard Headquarters, I meet my new boss and his second in command. My boss was Chief, Auxiliary and Education Division, which was part of the Office of Boating Safety. As Chief, Operations and Member Training Branch, my job was to develop and oversee a systematic training program for the Coast Guard Auxiliary. This was based on the position paper that I had written back in Salt Lake City. I was given a small office with one other officer. For a secretary I would share a clerk/typist with officers in another Branch. I did not need much space since I would be working with national level Auxiliary officers. Some of these volunteers were local to Washington but most were located at various places around the country. I found I would spend a lot of time on the phone, although I did have to travel to work out some problems.

The best tool I had to work with was a Wang Word Processer. This was the forerunner of the word processing program we have on our computer today. The Wang was a separate machine all by itself and was about the size of a ladies dressing table. Correcting mistakes and making wording changes was so much easier on the Wang than on a typewriter.

My first step consisted of overseeing the development of an outline of work that needed to be accomplished. The project was to develop training materials that were to be used to train Auxiliarist in three areas, boating safety education, vessel equipment inspection and operations. Training for these tasks were already being done, but in an unorganized manner and not always the same nationwide. Next came researching the information and conducting a nationwide search to locate experienced Auxiliarist to write the materials. Once the material was written, it was brought to Headquarters and the material was reviewed by Headquarters staff to be sure the material followed Coast Guard policy. Then it had to be typed and organized in a training booklet format. Then gallery prints were sent back to the Auxiliarist to be checked for errors or omissions.

The next step was to send the manuscripts to the Government Printing Office to be typeset and printed. After the booklets were typeset, there was another round of checking galleries for errors. Once the materials were printed, they would be shipped out as needed by the Government Printing Office.

While the training materials were being developed, my boss, Chief Auxiliary Office was working with the Auxiliary National Commodore to develop policy on how the training materials were to be used on the local level. Not all my time was spent of the educational project. There were always staff meetings, consulting with other departments on policy questions and numerous collateral duties.

Most people, I had served with in the Coast Guard, did not like the idea of being stationed in Washington, D.C. Living in a large city, fighting traffic, and putting up with the congestion just did not set well with people use to living near the coast or out at sea. I was not very happy about the idea either, but that that was where I was assigned.

By the time my tour in D.C. ended I would have twenty years in the Coast Guard. On the trip east Linda and I had been discussing when I would retire and where we wanted to live. One of the locations was West Virginia. This location came up because the state exempted military retirement pay form income tax. After much discussion, my wife and I decided to look for a residence in Charles Town, WV. From there I could commute to D.C. To get to work I would drive to Point of Rocks, MD and catch a commuter train.

Linda and I rented a two-story brick house in the older section of Charles Town. The house was old enough that it had a carriage barn in the back yard. I remember being close to a cemetery with tomb stones that were dated in the 1700s. The children loved the house. It was located near schools and there were a lot of other children, there age, for them to play with. We only lived in the house for about five months. The owner of the house sold out and the new owners wanted to move in right away before winter arrived. In the long run this worked out best for us. Later I found out the house, while looking good on the outside, was not insulated well and it cost over $600 a month to heat the place. I found a mobile home on the edge of town to rent.

The commute to D.C. was long, about 70 miles, so it took a good while to get to work. Once I got to Union Station, I still had to get to Coast Guard Headquarters building at Bussard Point on the Anacostia River. On the first day I went to make the commute I found the parking lot at the train station was full. It seems a lot of people had the same idea as I. I enjoyed the commute, but it made for a long day. My wife was not real pleased since I left early and arrived home late. It did not leave a lot of time to do chores at home.

After living in Charles Town for about a year I decided West Virginia was not the place for me. It seemed like every weekend the volunteer fire department was having a "fill the boot" drive to raise money for operating expenses. This and some other items made me realize that I would rather live in a state that had higher taxes than one that had trouble funding public utilities.

After much discussion we decided to move across the state line to Virginia. We rented a two-story farmhouse that was surrounded by fields. The address was a hamlet called White Post. This was a wide spot in the road with a country store and a white signpost in the center of a crossroad's intersection. There was our house and two or three other homes within a quarter mile distance from the intersection.

I would drive a short distance to Highway 60. There I would meet a lady from Winchester, VA and we would commute 70 miles to Washington. We had a location to leave a car and would take turns driving to work. Later, a couple of other gentlemen joined the carpool. With the traffic in D.C., it would take me two hours to get to work.

On snow days we could be almost to the city when they would announce, essential government workers only. Essential workers we were not. We would go on to work while people that live only a mile or so from work would get a snow day.

Because they're so many government workers in D.C., startling and quitting times were staggered to help cut down on congestion. One winter day, during an extra heavy snowfall, all workers were told to go home at 3 p.m. There were four of us at that time, but one of us worked downtown near the White House. By the time everyone was in the car, the streets of D.C. were hopelessly clogged. After two and half hours we were still not across the Potomac River. That usually took less than half hour. We decided to pull into a restraint for supper and wait for traffic to clear. It was very late when I got home that night.

Twice a year the Auxiliary would hold a national conference. The National Commodore and his staff, the District Commodores, and staff from each District, the Chief of Auxiliary and staff from each Coast Guard District and the Headquarters Chief of Auxiliary and staff would get together to review new policies and procedures. A lot of training was done at this time. Each conference was held in a different location. This would give local Auxiliarist an opportunity to meet the national staff and to get to know one another.

I got to see a lot of major cities in the U.S. during my three years. It was interesting to see the difference between the cities, yet in a lot of ways they were the same. I remember flying into Los Angeles, CA. and looking out the plane windows at the spaghetti mix of roadways and thinking that boy I did not want to drive in that mess. Little did I know that four years after I retired, I would visit LA once a week.

After three years at CG Headquarters, I was approaching my twenty-year mark of my service. After discussions with my wife, I decided to submit my letter requesting retirement. The Deputy chief Auxiliary tried to talk me out of submitting my request. He stated that if I stayed in a little longer, I would be able to advance to Commander. It was a promising idea, but it was not for me. There is a saying in the business world that a person raises to his level of incompetence. I felt that I had reached my level of incompetence and it was time to move on to other endeavors. I received my retirement letter with the separation date of September 30, 1979.

When my retirement date arrived, my coworkers held a retirement party. CG Headquarters was located next Fort McNair, and Army base located on the Anacostia River. The party was held at the officer's club. There were cocktails, a meal and of course the obligatory retirement cake. I was presented with a reproduction "Ships Wheel" with a plaque showing name and date as a parting gift.

Printed in the United States
by Baker & Taylor Publisher Services